Taunton's

Bathroom
IDEA BOOK

Taunton's

Bathroom

IDEA BOOK

SANDRA S. SORIA

The Taunton Press

The Taunton Press
Inspiration for hands-on living®

The Taunton Press, Inc.
63 South Main Street, PO Box 5506
Newtown, CT 06470-5506
e-mail: tp@taunton.com

Editor: Jennifer Renjilian Morris
Copy editor: Marc Sichel
Indexer: Jay Kreider
Jacket/Cover design: Kimberly Adis
Interior design: Kimberly Adis
Layout: David Giammattei
Illustrators: Jean Tuttle and courtesy of Kohler Co.
Front cover photographers: Jo-Ann Richards (left); Ryann Ford (top right);
Hulya Kolabas (bottom right)
Back cover photographers: Eric Roth (top right); Doug Smith (center right);
Eric Roth (bottom right); Hulya Kolabas (bottom left)

The following names/manufacturers appearing in *Bathroom Idea Book* are trademarks:
American Standard Brands®, Bakelite®, Corian®, DuPont®, Durock®, ENERGY STAR®,
Habitat for Humanity® ReStore®, Kohler®, Lucite®, WaterSense®, Wonder Board®

Library of Congress Cataloging-in-Publication Data
Soria, Sandra S.
  Bathroom idea book / Sandra S. Soria.
      pages cm
  ISBN 978-1-60085-520-7
1. Bathrooms. 2. Interior decoration. I. Title.
  NK2117.B33S6725 2013
  747.7'8--dc23
                                    2012051218

Printed in the United States of America
10 9 8 7 6 5 4 3 2

acknowledgments

MY THANKS GO OUT TO ALL THE talented, creative people that lent their work to the making of this book. To my editors, Carolyn Mandarano and Jennifer Renjilian Morris, whose clear and patient guidance on matters large and small, visual and written made this edition better in so many ways.

The images in this volume are both gorgeous and informative, culled from the most intriguing and well-designed homes across the country. Without the skill and aesthetic of the dozens of photographers, interior designers, architects, and builders that contributed their work to this project it would not be in your hands today. Photo editor Erin Giunta has managed the hundreds of images for the book, and David Giammattei laid out the book, putting the photographs into the eye-pleasing order you find them here.

My appreciation extends to the technical advisors and advice shared by many bathroom industry experts—from manufacturers, interior designers, and builders to associations and remodeling professionals. I learned so much about the state of the American bathroom today, and had a lot of fun doing it.

And, always, to my husband, sons, and other dear ones . . . thanks for putting up with me through the ups and downs of researching, writing, and gathering materials for what I hope is a helpful, easy-to-read, and relatable guide for all.

contents

introduction

I'S ONLY BEEN A MERE 100 YEARS since indoor plumbing reached into American homes via a sanitary system of pipes and drains. My mom, now 75 years young, didn't see it come to her rural Iowa farmhouse until she was a teenager. Before that, it was chamber pots, outhouses, and baths in galvanized tubs every Saturday night.

Of course, elegant Victorian-era homes in the rapidly growing cities at the turn of the last century beat the rural farmhouse to the punch. Many turned unused bedrooms into grand bathing and dressing areas that included enamel tubs (luxuriously sized at 5 ft. long), pedestal sinks, and water closets with siphon jets.

The real gusher of change came in the 25 years between 1929 and 1954, when sales of plumbing supplies grew 350 percent to a multibillion-dollar industry. Postwar housing booms brought the advent of the tract house and the spread of the suburbs, when the bathroom was a small, utilitarian speck on the American floor plan, leaving more square footage for two or three bedrooms and 2.5 children. Now, the United States Census Bureau tells us that 57 percent of single-family houses built since 2002 have three or more bathrooms.

It's no big mystery why the bathroom has stepped up to take a more prominent place in the home. It's a high-value room for busy

modern families whose days are jam-packed with work, school, and activities. Whether we're getting ready for the day or unwinding after it's done, a personal space with a checklist of your favorite updated amenities is an everyday getaway that's good for body and soul.

Manufacturers, in turn, have stepped up to fill the demand for more and more elaborate bathrooms with shapely fixtures, chic surfacing, and high-tech function that make it as rewarding to design or remodel a bathroom as it is to come home to the finished space.

Still, designing a bathroom can be a daunting process given all the choices in products and the technical nature of plumbing. Enter *Bathroom Idea Book*. Its

goal is to break down the steps of planning, building, and finishing a bathroom into a logical process that leads you from start to finish. More than 350 images will inspire you along the way, presenting thousands of pretty and practical ideas—for all budgets—that will help you realize your own vision for an efficient and pampering space.

planning for the bed bath

● ● ●

THE BATHROOM IS ONE OF THE SMALLEST ROOMS IN THE HOUSE, YET the most hardworking. This little utilitarian space hasn't always gotten the design attention it deserves. But that's no longer true. Today, standard fixtures and surfaces are moving aside for sleek silhouettes, efficient functioning, and intriguing materials. Choice abounds, which makes the homeowner's job more challenging, but a lot more fun, too.

With all the goodies available to you, the last thing you want is to be harried into a decision in the home improvement aisle or during a fast-moving meeting with your contractor. As with most home endeavors, the best place to start envisioning your new bath is on paper. Whether you're creating a new bathroom or updating an existing one, planning is essential. Gather a notebook of information and inspiration, taking color copies or tearsheets from books and magazines. Visit home stores and Web sites for brochures and printouts of what's in the marketplace.

As you get a feel for what's out there, think about how you want your bath to look and feel as well as function. Of course, the bath needs to do what it's always done — accommodate the basic hygienic needs of your family. But today's bath functions as an everyday retreat as well. Is it more important that your bath energizes you for

the morning rush or relaxes you after a long day? How will the room need to perform and for whom? A hardworking kids' bath, a gracious guest bath, or a master suite? This chapter will help you answer these questions and guide you as you make decisions about your space's looks, layout, and level of luxury.

Sparkly surfaces and airy colors make a bathroom look bigger and feel calmer. Pale water hues, touches of glass, and crisp white trim make a spa statement in this small bath.

budgeting

● ● ● ENVISIONING A NEW BATH IS A FUN, creative process. Sure it's OK to dream big…as long as you keep reality in mind. Consider first what can't be changed—most likely the size of your budget and the space itself. You'll save money in the end with careful thought and planning at the start because you'll avoid having to make hasty decisions on big-ticket items during the building process—and costly redos if things don't run smoothly.

RIGHT Small soaking tubs are less expensive to buy and use than large jetted models. This slender built-in tub with its narrow ledge leaves room for a spacious glass shower booth.

BELOW Free-standing tubs molded in acrylic and resins are bringing designer style to a broader market. These sculptural and flexible pieces allow for creative layouts and eye-grabbing looks.

Save money on a bath redo by showcasing expensive tile in a limited area. By saving money with laminate tile flooring and a beadboard wainscot, this homeowner could splurge on pretty glass tile in the standard-size shower.

•dollars and sense

A well-designed, updated bath is a high-value room—from the perspective of both homeowner and homebuyer. But it's never a good idea to over-improve your home for the market or your neighborhood. For better or worse, how elaborately you update is linked to the real estate picture—if you want to see a return on that investment.

When home prices are soft, it's harder to recoup those remodeling dollars if you sell your home. The market will go up and down, but an old rule of thumb still holds: If you are

planning to stay in your house for another 10 years, upgrade away. If not, consider what changes you can make on a budget. The investment, after all, is no small one. These days, the average cost for a midrange bath remodel is $15,000. Factor in high-end fixtures and finishes, and the average cost jumps to more than $30,000. If you have to alter your plumbing lines, move interior walls, or bump out an exterior wall to make room for the bath of your dreams, plan on closer to $50,000.

TOP LEFT Just a few elegant touches can make a basic bathroom sparkle. Ebony-framed mirrors visually link to a dark-stained wood floor and bring design focus to the mostly white room. A gilt mirror and silk sconce punctuate the style.

ABOVE Consider borrowing space from the bedroom next door if a master bathroom will increase your home's value and your happiness. This pretty space updated a classic '50s ranch, which was stuck in the past with its three bedrooms and one small shared bath.

LEFT A limited budget doesn't have to cramp your style. A combination bath and shower is made more fun with a tent-like shower curtain suspended from a standard track found at hospital-supply stores.

FACING PAGE Classic materials and a soft color palette will ensure a bathroom's appeal for a longer stretch of time. Timeless hexagon mosaic tile and marble mark this room as traditional; modern hinged-glass shower doors and soft blue paint freshen the look for today's tastes.

•the budget-conscious bath

A cosmetic update is another way to go. This generally includes paint, updated faucets and lighting, new accessories (such as knobs, mirrors, and towel rods), a new floor or shower wall, and one new fixture. Small-scale bathroom projects can come in under $5,000, especially if you do the work yourself or can accomplish the remodel without hiring a contractor.

Save money by selecting products carefully. A pedestal sink will save both dollars and space in small baths. Well-sealed hardwood floors look rich but are less expensive than installing tile.

More about...
BUDGET-HAPPY BATHROOM IDEAS

Losing a grip on the budget is a homeowner's biggest fear. Here are some ways to keep costs in hand.

Dig in. Even if you aren't Picasso with the grouting gun, there are a lot of ways you can do some of the work on your bath and save big bucks. Most common? Do the demolition yourself and haul away the debris. And at the other end of the project, do some finishing work, such as painting or simple tile installation.

Buy it yourself. Talk to your contractor about purchasing your own fixtures. Contractors mark up the cost of fixtures about 10 percent to cover their costs in buying and retrieving the items. Shop for deals and do the legwork to save dollars.

Don't move walls or fixtures. If it's possible to stick with the same footprint and floor plan, you will instantly pare thousands of dollars from the overall cost.

Consider labor costs. For many bathroom items, the price tag is just the start. Be sure to factor in the cost of installing specialty fixtures or tile—two big money grabbers.

Opt to redo rather than replace. For instance, reglazing an enamel tub saves hundred of dollars over replacing it.

ABOVE Stock cabinetry and solid-core counters with integrated sinks are a contemporary way to keep the budget happy. For more savings, stick with open-shelf storage over built-in cupboards.

RIGHT Think outside the box to avoid a boring bathroom. A stainless-steel utility sink and inexpensive subway tile create an industrial chic look that is a breeze to keep clean.

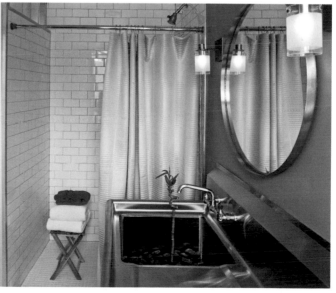

ABOVE Mosaic tiles are sold by the square foot affixed to mesh sheets, which saves hundreds of dollars in labor costs. By keeping the original tub, these owners could splurge on fresh tile, a new stock cabinet with a solid-core sink and counter, and a water-saving toilet.

FACING PAGE Refurbished vintage fixtures cost far less than buying new, and they can have more personality. Vinyl-sheet flooring in a classic basketweave pattern underscores the cottage charm of this guest bath, but at a lower price point than tile.

For a look that will stay fresh over time, think simple and clean. White cabinetry and classic hexagon floor tile won't look dated, effectively stretching your decorating dollars.

picking the right pro

●●● UNLESS YOU ARE A SEASONED AND confident do-it-yourselfer, an extensive bathroom remodel is best left to the professionals. Architects and general contractors will be familiar with the building codes and the process of obtaining a building permit, which varies from municipality to municipality. Permits are generally required when structural work is involved or the basic living areas of a home are changed. Depending on the size and complexity of your project, consider calling in an expert, especially one who can show you a portfolio of successful bathroom projects. Remember to get at least three estimates for your project to be sure you are getting the most for your budget.

TYPES OF REMODELING PROFESSIONALS

a general contractor can handle modest home improvements that don't demand professional design services. Seek out an experienced, local home contractor. Check with your local Better Business Bureau or Consumer Affairs office to be certain there are no complaints on record for the contractor. Also, most states require contractors to be licensed and/or bonded and to carry insurance for workers' compensation, property damage, and personal liability. Ask to see a copy of the contractor's license and insurance policy.

A **design/build contractor** provides design and construction services in the same company. This specialty contractor can see your project through from start to finish. Find these services at home improvement centers and specialty design shops.

An **architect** is an asset on large remodeling projects that require construction drawings. Investing in the design and engineering phase of your project will help you define its parameters and costs. Find a licensed architect who is experienced with remodeling and can anticipate the challenges that can pop up when you're working within an existing structure.

TOP When a bathroom remodel involves bumping out space or borrowing it from another room, it's best to tap the expertise of an architect or bath designer. By placing the shower on a diagonal, this designer made efficient use of space and complemented the sloping lines of the dormered room.

LEFT Professional designers will help you integrate your bath design with the rest of your architecture. Though small, this bathroom has big style thanks to clever choices—such as natural wood paneling installed horizontally that blends with the eco-modern feel of the home.

FACING PAGE When you buy stock or semi-custom cabinetry at home improvement centers or bath specialty shops, you can take advantage of the design services they offer. Designers guide you in picking a palette and surface materials, as well as consult on creative solutions for more storage and style.

what about your needs?

● ● ● THE PLANNING PHASE IS THE TIME TO THINK about who will be using the space and how. What are the priorities for the bathroom? This information will help you target your dollars to your priorities. For instance, if the room will serve as a busy hub for the family in the morning, then layout and safe, durable surfaces are important features. If you're looking to update a guest bath that sees little use, design might trump durability. Maybe you've been dreaming of a pampering place to unwind at the end of the day? In that case, a few luxuries such as a steam shower or soaking tub might bubble up to the top of your list.

Bathrooms break down into a few common categories: master bath, family bath, guest bath, children's bath, and powder room. The following pages will help you decide what features you want to include in your home.

TOP A cushioned spot to apply cosmetics can make a girl's day, every day. This one bridges two separate vanities to make the best use of space and keep the overall look clean and serene.

ABOVE Think about the amenities that would improve your daily routine. This small television is tucked into a strip of linen storage, ready to present the news, stock reports, or classic entertainment during morning prep time.

LEFT Are you a shower person but your partner prefers a long soak in a warm tub? A walk-in shower that falls in line with the tub's width makes the most of the space in this galley-style bathroom.

FACING PAGE Create a spa ambiance in your bath by keeping color subdued and adding a few extras. A jetted tub and steam shower make this a relaxing spot. Candles and natural stone finishes please the senses.

the master bath

●●● THERE IS NOT A MORE PERSONAL ROOM ON THE American home's floor plan than the master bathroom. And the space has long hovered around the top of the list for the most popular room to remodel. Maybe it's the allure of all the new designs and tempting extras for the bath, or that busy modern lives demand an everyday sanctuary. Whatever the reason, having an updated, pampering master bath is a top priority.

The master bath has gone way beyond the utilitarian space it once was. Amenities at all price points up the spa factor of any size room. Some of the most popular features are small steam showers, deep soaking tubs, sound and video systems, towel-warming drawers, and radiant-heat floors.

These extras are tempting, but they need to be planned for. Steam showers require moisture-proof surfaces or a heavy-duty ventilation system, for instance. Good planning also helps you decide where you can save elsewhere in your project so you can splurge on a few items.

Frameless showers make use of relatively new technology in sturdy hinges and tempered glass. Though a big-ticket item, these glass panels cut down on tiling and construction costs.

LEFT These days, master bathrooms are indulgent spaces with spa-inspired amenities. This bath offers up a steam shower, soaking tub, and a modern, two-way gas fireplace that warms the master bedroom while it heats up the bathroom.

BELOW Shower/tub combinations are taking smart new forms these days. In this master bathroom, the bathtub surround doubles as a bench in the shower for a clever use of space.

planning a master bath

The most popular and effective layout for a shared master bath is one that allows two people to enjoy the space together while providing private areas for individual matters. Planning a separate area for the toilet or placing dual sinks on opposite ends of the room, for instance, are small changes that will make morning rush hours and nighttime relaxing hours more efficient.

Before you meet with a contractor or architect, sit down with your partner to compare notes on wants and necessities in a shared space. Consider not only what new amenities you'd like to include in this room, but also think about what doesn't work with your current bath.

Borrowed from the Japanese bathing tradition, small but deep tubs are finding their way into American baths. Though it actually takes up less floor space, this tall tub offers full immersion for a relaxing soak. The tubs are offered with or without jets, and many homeowners are opting for the quiet simplicity of a spray-free bath.

Think about ways to add efficiency to the morning routine. Here, a jetted tub is centered between the shower and water closet, offering distinct activity zones and a sense of privacy for all.

ABOVE A successful master bath plan makes room for two people to move throughout the space and offers privacy zones. This room features a wide center walkway that divides grooming and bathing areas. A water closet cleverly made with two panes of translucent glass offers stylish seclusion.

LEFT A steam shower is an increasingly popular amenity in the master suite. This one is big enough to fit two people and includes a bench to fully enjoy the experience.

a compact family bath

●●● THE SIZE OF THE AMERICAN HOME HAS ballooned over the years. In the 1950s, families made do in about 1,000 sq. ft. Though house size has taken a dip during the current roller-coaster real estate market, today's families are still stretching out in homes two and a half times that size. Back then, it was common for families to share a single main bath instead of the 2.5 bathrooms inside many homes today.

Today, durability, ease of cleaning, and storage are at the top of the priorities list for a compact family bath. For durable, easy-clean finishes and fixtures, check out acrylic or solid-surface products, which are more mold- and mildew-resistant than ceramic or stone. Faucets in satin finishes are less demanding than shiny chrome types that show watermarks and fingerprints.

TOP LEFT When space is an issue, consider trading in the typical tub/shower combination for a well-appointed shower. With the addition of a hand sprayer, this shower makes it easier to bathe young children.

TOP RIGHT A shared bath in an older home is often small, but it doesn't have to be dull. Treat a vintage bath to a fresh tile treatment and shower curtain for a brighter start to the day.

LEFT Rounded edges and easy-to-clean surfaces make good partners in a hardworking family bath. To ease the budget, use tile strategically, mixing different types in complementary colors for design impact.

FACING PAGE Hinged panels of glass set a sleek stage for a family bath that includes a traditional tub/shower combination. Porthole windows and a rainfall showerhead add fun and function to the space.

ABOVE Help a small bath appear larger—and more glamorous—with creamy hues and plenty of light. Whitewashed river stone flooring and modern woods decked out in ivory are set to a glow by circular, frosted-glass cutouts.

RIGHT Borrow the European concept of an open shower to make a tiny bath accessible. Completely tiled walls and floor, plus stainless-steel fixtures, make this entire bath a waterproof shower stall. Otherwise, the room would be too small to accommodate bathing.

TOP LEFT Streamline with a pint-sized potty to give the illusion of more space. A glass shower screen or shower door puts up no visual roadblocks that would further chop up a tight space. The tile design continues into the shower to visually elongate the space.

ABOVE A petite bathroom has plenty of room for a few little luxuries. A ceiling-mounted rain showerhead is a smart solution for a small shower stall because it directs water straight down to minimize splash and make better use of a tiny area.

LEFT Because it's not used as often, you can indulge a small, secondary bath with surfaces such as glass and stone that require more care when used daily. This sleek glass counter appears to float between the shower and wall of this chic but diminutive bath. The glass requires only a regular dusting to keep it looking good between uses.

Limiting pattern in a small bath establishes a serene scheme. For interest, layer on a mix of textures from nubby to high gloss. A basket that keeps tissue close at hand and a gleaming ceramic stool for a bathing caddy add visual interest and a few creature comforts.

the guest bath

●●● GUEST BATHS BY DEFINITION PULL ONLY part-time duty. If you're lucky enough to count one among your home's rooms, comfort should be its main goal. Whether your guest bath sees only sporadic visitors or a regular rotation of family and friends, think about how you can make the room accommodating and welcoming.

To get started, remember what the most gracious and memorable inns you've visited have in common—fluffy towels, a basket of sundries, and hooks for hanging personal items. Flattering lighting, a cosmetic color palette, and open storage that keeps essentials close at hand also show thoughtful planning. Most people don't go all-out on these secondary bath spaces, so select items that can be easily spruced up on a moment's notice.

LEFT Put hotel style and comfort in your guest bath with classic materials and special extras. Marble, mirror, and subway tile are elegant choices. The handheld shower adds an extra dimension of bathing luxury.

BELOW A cramped bath can still extend a gracious welcome to guests. Keep bathing essentials in view and within reach on a convenient shelf. Wood tones make the space warm and inviting.

gallery

guest baths

Think about all the little extras you get excited to find in a hotel bathroom, then add them to your guest bath to pamper the people that pass through your home.

RIGHT The right mix of open and closed storage will keep your bath tidy and at the ready for last-minute guests. Look for readymade cabinetry with mix-and-match components that fit your needs and your space.

BOTTOM RIGHT Add drama in a small bathroom with paint and lighting. This garnet shade is complementary to skin tones, and warm and enveloping in mood. Recessed and spot lighting work with mirrored and marble surfaces to bring light and sparkle.

BOTTOM LEFT Plush towels plus special soap and bath products will make guests feel pampered. Resting on a sleek, waterproof shower stool, a bright, white towel is a smart little investment in your guest's comfort.

LEFT A gracious guest bath has thoughtful touches. A simple shield-back chair adds not only classical design but also a practical place for a guest to put on makeup or pull on a pair of socks. A textural area rug warms the tile floor and the tranquil pale blue and white palette.

BELOW Keep all the necessary elements of a pleasant overnight stay close at hand for your guests. Bath basics and indulgent sundries are within sight in this graphic open shelving.

the kids' bath

●●● SAFETY IS JOB ONE FOR A ROOM THAT contains lots of water and energetic children. Besides making sure surfaces are slip-proof, choosing finishes that are durable and easy to clean is also an important consideration.

A bath designed for children should also have some fun. Creating a space that draws the kids in makes bathing routines easier for parents, and it gives kids ownership over the space as well. When you're planning a bath for young people, start by looking at the space from their point of view…literally. Try lowering your sight line to a child's eye level to get a sense of how they see and navigate the space. Put the most colorful aspects of the design where they can see it. Establish low drawers for a child's personal items or a stool to boost them to sink level. If two or more children share a space, creating separate drawers, hooks, or towels will encourage a sense of pride in home and self.

This Jack and Jill bathroom is cleverly joined at the shared shower. Frosted shower doors close to offer privacy for the bather and both wings of the bath.

ABOVE For a bath that will be current for a longer period of time, choose patterns that appeal to different ages. In fresh, soft colors, these stripes work for a young child but won't turn off a teenager.

FACING PAGE BOTTOM For kids' baths that see a lot of action, borrow ideas from the locker room. This creative family made sure that more than one child can get ready at a time by installing two of everything. The commercial shower stalls set the scene. A series of mirrors over the sinks and the center vanity provide separate grooming spots.

It doesn't take much to make a child's bathroom a happy place. Fun patterns and accessories will draw young ones in at bath time; a vinyl floor with texture and a matte finish will keep them from slipping along the way.

More about...
AVOIDING DANGER IN THE BATH

the danger of electrocution makes water and electricity a dangerous—and potentially lethal—combination in the bath. Here are ways to keep this family space safe.

- Install GFCI (ground fault circuit interrupter) devices in the bathroom to protect people from severe electrical shocks. A GFCI-protected outlet is essentially an inexpensive electric receptacle that's used in place of standard outlets. It will break the circuit if it detects problems in the current.

- Use vapor-tight recessed lights in the shower area. Problems arise when steam or water comes in contact with a typical recessed fixture.

- Unplug small electrical appliances when they're not in use.

- Avoid using portable heaters or fans in a bathroom. If it's necessary to use these devices, make sure they're plugged in to a GFCI-protected outlet.

For more information, visit the U.S. Consumer Product Safety Commission at http://www.cpsc.gov.

powder rooms

●●● THE PINT-SIZE DIMENSIONS OF A POWDER room, or half-bath, pose an obvious design challenge. Often located off a main hallway or a public space, the perfect powder room also needs to offer its visitors privacy. And its design should flow easily from the rest of the house. This is no small feat in a room that averages 20 sq. ft. in floor space.

When pulling together a powder room, layer on sound-absorbing textiles for a buffer of privacy. When deciding on colors and surfaces, you should obviously consider the feel you want to create, but also take cues from surrounding rooms. You do not want this very public place to stand out as an oddball to the rest of your home.

ABOVE A vanity with the look of freestanding furniture is perfect in a powder room that is adjacent to living areas. Bronze finishes and iridescent mosaic tile underscore the room's elegance.

LEFT Small, wall-mounted vanities slip easily into narrow half-baths. This modern vanity is capped with a vertical mirror to highlight the extra space provided by high ceilings. Pale purple paint on both the walls and moldings makes the room feel more contemporary and dramatic.

Contrary to design myth, lyrical patterns can be used successfully in tight spaces. A strip of white tile behind the vanity adds visual relief and highlights an elegant small vanity and smoked-glass sink.

ABOVE Farmhouse style is all about simple charm and resourcefulness. A vintage utility sink that has been freshly resurfaced is both fun and functional in a modern country house.

LEFT Don't let an itty-bitty space cramp your style. While this tree-pattern wallpaper would be too much of a good thing in a larger room, it's the right dose of fun in a small bathroom—especially when it playfully mimics the wooded lot beyond the window.

working with your space

●●●

ONCE YOU'VE FIGURED OUT THE PARAMETERS OF YOUR BATHROOM space and how it will be used (and by whom), you're ready to start plotting out what goes where within the room. The best way to start planning the layout, or floor plan, is on paper. Graph paper, pencils, and a ruler will be important tools in this phase of the project. You don't need the drafting skills of Frank Lloyd Wright to work this puzzle, but you do need to know some basic bath arrangement guidelines. These specifications will help you plan a bathroom that is efficient, comfortable, and appealing to the eye.

If the placement of your fixtures is limited by plumbing concerns, consider those first, or discuss the cost of moving plumbing lines with your contractor to budget for the costs. As you research your options and play on paper, you'll discover there are many layout options within any size space, each with their own budget implications.

This chapter will cover basic room arrangement rules and specifications, as well as explore creative ways to work within different types of spaces. We'll also discuss ways to find existing space in your home to make way for the bathroom you're envisioning.

See-through shower stalls engineered with panes of tempered glass and held by narrow channels or simple hinges are opening up today's bathroom designs. The easily sealed chamber can be converted to a steam shower—one of the top five luxuries on the home decorator's wish list.

floor plan options

THERE ARE MULTIPLE PRINTED AND ONLINE sources for bathroom floor plans. The National Kitchen and Bath Association (NKBA) is one multipronged site that offers resources and information for consumers who are in the throes of a bathroom project. The NKBA provides information on planning a space that considers both user comfort and standard building codes.

Several common floor plans for baths of all sizes are shown on the facing page. Narrow your choices to those that best fit your situation. Review these basic guidelines before you put pencil to paper to determine what elements your room can handle and how to best organize them.

For more privacy in a shared bath, use partial walls to create separate chambers. Clad in chic dark walnut, this contemporary wall and vanity combination provides a beautiful buffer for the tub and shower areas.

SMALL FULL BATH

Super small baths are limited to combination shower/tub units.

40 sq. ft.

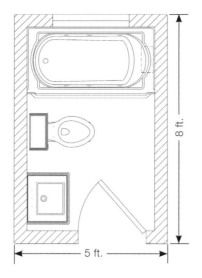

UNUSUAL LAYOUT

Compact bathrooms still leave room for dramatic layouts. Surrounded by a partial wall, a center tub can be a pretty focal point and help block the commode for privacy. The layout works without the wall, too.

110 sq. ft.

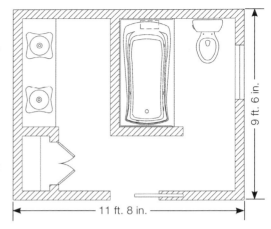

SEPARATE TUB AND SHOWER

This amount of space is the minimum for separate tub and shower.

85 sq. ft.

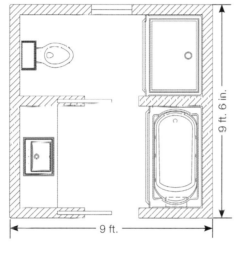

MAKE THE MOST OF THE SPACE

A corner shower unit leaves more clearance room for the commode and tub.

101 sq. ft.

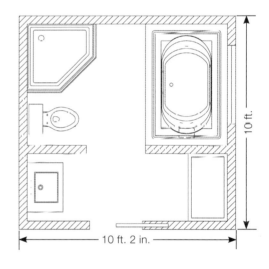

PRIVATE SPACES

Put a shower and the commode in the same water closet to create a bathroom within a bathroom for added privacy in a two-person bath.

178 sq. ft.

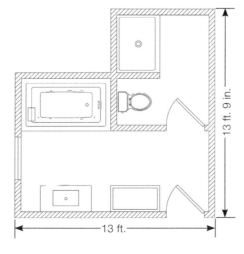

L-SHAPED ROOMS

Many bathrooms occupy L-shaped spaces in the home. This type of space allows for ample vanity space and a private commode area. A freestanding or round tub would also work.

177 sq. ft.

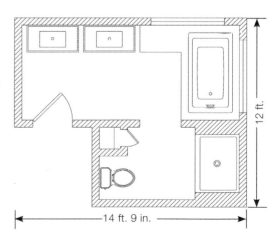

planning clearance for fixtures

● ● ● THERE ARE MINIMUM SPACE REQUIREMENTS that can dictate the placement of each fixture within your planned bathroom space. These standards are based on comfortable and safe use for everyone within the space.

Building code standards must be considered as well. Though most municipalities have chosen to adopt national standards as their model for local codes, some codes still vary from municipality to municipality. Any contractor you choose should be well versed in your local codes and be able to provide the codes in written form to you.

The minimum size for a full bath (with a bathtub, toilet, and lavatory) is 5 ft. x 7 ft. With the addition of 1 ft. more (5 ft. x 8 ft.), though, you'll have a much wider selection of bathtubs and lavatories. A powder room usually has only two fixtures—a toilet and lavatory—and can be created within a space as small as 54 in. x 48 in.

DOOR CLEARANCE

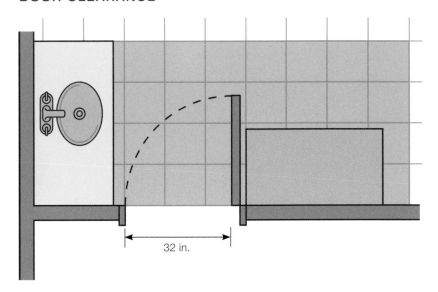

32 in.

Allow for at least a 32-in. doorway and for unobstructed clearance when the door is open at 90 degrees.

SINK PLACEMENT

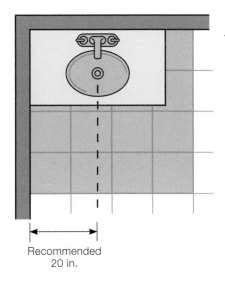

Recommended 20 in.

When positioning your sink, consider elbow room by measuring from the center of the basin to adjacent walls or obstacles. The distance should be 15 in. to 20 in. For a double sink, the distance between the centerlines of the two basins should be at least 36 in.

VANITY HEIGHT

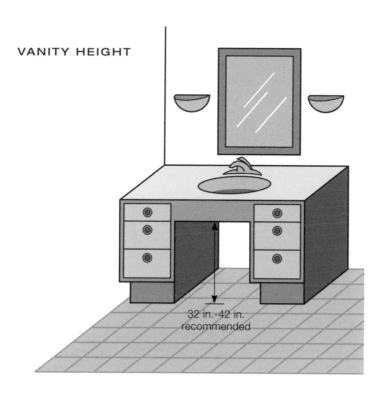

32 in.-42 in. recommended

Vanity height is an important issue and depends on the comfort of the user. Most users feel comfortable with a height between 34 in. and 42 in.

SHOWER SIZE

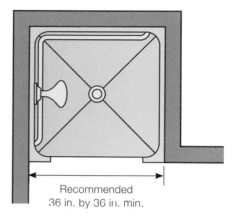

Recommended 36 in. by 36 in. min.

A shower requires a minimum of 36 in. x 36 in. For optimum comfort, consider more space.

TOILET PLACEMENT

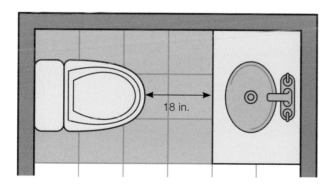

18 in.

For comfortable use of the toilet, the distance between the center of the toilet basin and any wall or fixture should be at least 15 in. To meet universal standards, minimum clear space in front of a toilet should be 30 in. x 48 in., but a 48-in. x 48-in. floor space from the front edge of the toilet to any wall or fixture opposite it is a more accessible and desirable minimum.

CEILING HEIGHT

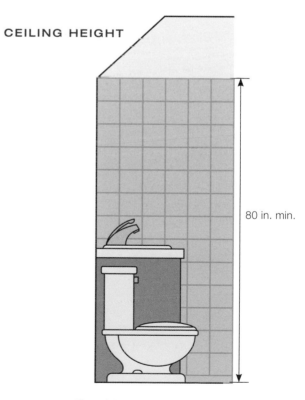

80 in. min.

The minimum ceiling height is 80 in. when the ceiling is over a fixture. Shower heights should be 80 in. as well.

universal design

● ● ● AS YOU PLOT OUT YOUR NEW BATHROOM, keep the present and future needs of all family members in mind. Physical needs can change. Whether due to a temporary impairment, such as minor surgery, or a permanent disability, you or one of your loved ones may be faced with physical changes and challenges in the future. The simple process of aging naturally increases our dependence on others. Caring for an elderly parent can bring these issues into focus sooner rather than later. By working some of the principles of universal design into your project now, you'll be able to move through these potential changes and still enjoy equal access and independence.

Roomy showers with low to no threshold accommodate users of all ages and abilities.
The handheld shower slides along a stainless pole for use by people of multiple heights.
Cutouts under the vanity sink allow access for chairs and wheelchairs.

TOP LEFT Borrow an idea from European designers and install a shower floor contiguous with the bathroom floor. This ebony ceramic tile adds both style and function. Add 18-in.-high benches for safety and comfort.

ABOVE Grab bars add safety to any bathroom. This modern bathroom has plenty of grips, plus easy-to-use drawer pulls.

LEFT Nonslip floor surfaces make sense in a bathroom designed for all. Natural stone tiles, such as this slate, don't sacrifice style for safety.

•details of universal design

It's more cost-effective to incorporate universal design features in the planning phases of a project, when they can be added at little or no extra cost. Incorporating the features during a remodeling or building project will preclude the need for retrofits later, which are always more costly.

Little touches can mean a lot of comfort in a bathroom. In this glam space, sturdy towel racks, an easy-to-reach faucet located outside the shower stall, and a mirror designed to tip for various heights add up to accessibility.

More about...
BASICS OF
UNIVERSAL DESIGN

by definition, universal design is "the creation of products and environments meant to be usable by all people, to the greatest extent possible, without the need for adaptation or specialization." Here's what that means in layman's terms.

- Provide the same means of use for all users: identical whenever possible, equivalent when not.
- Accommodate right- or left-handed access and use.
- The design minimizes hazards and the adverse consequences of accidental or unintended actions.
- The design can be used efficiently and comfortably and with a minimum of fatigue. For instance, it allows the user to maintain a neutral body position.
- Appropriate size and space is provided for approach, reach, manipulation, and use regardless of the user's body size, posture, or mobility.
- Provide a clear line of sight to important elements for any seated or standing user.
- Make reaching for all components comfortable for any seated or standing user.
- Provide adequate space for the use of assistive devices or personal assistance.

Good lighting is a safety factor in any room. Frosted glass diffuses the light in this accessible shower to a soft glow. Sleek grab bars don't spoil the modern mood in this marble, limestone, and teak bathroom.

finding the space

● ● ● WHEN YOU WANT TO CARVE OUT A NEW bath or expand an existing one, the most economical option is to borrow space from nearby rooms. Walk around your house with a creative eye. The first places to consider are closets, hallways, and empty corners that adjoin the bath space. Pay special attention to walls that back to the bathroom's "wet wall"—the wall that contains plumbing pipes. It's far less expensive to install fixtures if you can tap existing lines.

The main question is where you'll place the toilet. If a new fixture can be connected to the existing vent stack, you'll shave hundreds of dollars off of the remodeling bill. In a house with two or more stories, it's most cost-efficient to stack the bathrooms. This is something to keep in mind if you're planning to look up to the attic or down toward the basement for space to add a bathroom.

To create an airier master suite, open up the bathroom into the sleeping area. This trim tub takes only a sliver of space from the bedroom—even with its attached slice of wall— but allows for more floor space in the bath.

ABOVE Borrowing a closet niche from an adjoining den or bedroom can make way for a little luxury in the bath. A glass-top vanity and mirror make a sparkly, room-expanding primping station, with a little extra storage on the sides.

LEFT Small but elegant touches will add splash to a diminutive basement bath. Chrome hardware, wall-mounted faucets, and a marble threshold make a statement in this spare, full-function bathroom.

•found-space considerations

Most found space involves a compromise. Gain a bathroom, lose a closet, for instance. Think carefully about what tradeoffs you're willing to make. If a larger bathroom seems a happy switch for the linen closet in the hallway, make your move—but don't forget to plan storage within your new bath space to make up for the missing closet. Many homeowners co-opt an underused bedroom for a larger family bath or master suite. (Before you act, consider what losing a bedroom would do to your home's value!)

Once a second-story sunroom, this cottage-style bathroom has retained the abundant natural light of the original room. The free-standing enamel tub adds graceful curves to a bath marked by Shaker-style simplicity.

ABOVE Adding space to an existing bath sometimes starts at the doorway. An industrial roller system with a contemporary shed-style door doesn't require the clearance of a standard, open-in door.

TOP RIGHT Frameless glass shower stalls allow more design flexibility in small baths. This custom shower overlaps the tub deck to save some inches. Plus the stall can be designed to work with the high windows often found in remodeled basement baths.

More about...
TIPS FOR ADDING ON A BATHROOM

decide whether your existing space (and budget) provides for a half-bath or full bath. Have an idea of the floor plan and amenities you want to discuss with a contractor.

- Bathrooms are important to today's homebuyer. If you have too few baths compared to bedrooms or if you have a finished floor without a bath, then the added value to your home of a bathroom addition will likely pay for itself when it's time to sell.

- Having a new bath above, below, or adjacent to kitchen or laundry room plumbing will allow for shared pipes and drains, saving you lots of money on costly new fittings.

- Planning a new bathroom back to back with an existing one, where a plumbing wall can be shared, is the most affordable scenario.

- Current codes require an operable window or vent in every bathroom. Make sure this is possible in the space you're eyeing for a new bath.

• ideas for small baths

RIGHT Shed-roof porches or mudrooms can be incorporated into country-style bathrooms in older homes where bath space is at a premium. Frosted panes and beadboard paneling make an affordable backdrop for this vintage copper tub. A shapely modern acrylic tub can create the look for less.

BOTTOM RIGHT A vanity stripped of extraneous hardware—and even legs—will look tidy in a small space. A gooseneck faucet and slender mirror add visual height to this boxy room, while a corner shower buys needed floor space.

BELOW Don't fear using patterns with pizzazz in a small bathroom. Classic porcelain tile and hand-colored aviary wallpaper give this secondary bath more prominence. Adding a lot of white frames the pattern and makes the room appear bigger.

ABOVE Make the best use of a space by installing a bathtub inside the shower. Look for affordable marble look-alikes or sheet goods for the classic elegance of a Roman bath.

LEFT White tile or paint is a simple solution to a narrow bath. This room is bathed in white, except for a focal-point wall of mosaic tile. Centering the shower head and faucets on the long wall of the tub gives the user extra elbow room.

attic baths

● ● ● CHARACTER-LADEN ATTICS ARE READY environments for creating a bed-and-bath retreat. The biggest issue is figuring how to get water all the way up there and down again. Your best bet is to figure out where your plumbing is on the level below and design your attic bath directly above the existing bathroom. If things just aren't stacking up for you, consider raising the floor to house the plumbing. Just make sure to allow yourself enough headroom. Most codes dictate a minimum of 7½ ft. of headroom in at least 50 percent of what is termed "usable floor space." Usable floor space is typically defined as the portion of the room with headroom of at least 5 ft. from floor to ceiling.

It's important to consult with an architect or engineer before embarking on an attic bathroom addition. Ensure that the load-bearing capabilities of the roof system are not compromised by the additional weight of fixtures and water. Sometimes rafters and floor framing require reinforcement, which will also affect the finished headroom space (and the cost). Rafters will need to be inspected for any signs of stress or damage, including cracks, sagging, or insect damage.

ABOVE Many attics feature dormers, which can help add enough headroom when creating a small bathroom. In this old house, open shelving and an angled counter help ease the space constraints of this narrow dormer bath.

RIGHT Showers are easier than baths to install In an attic, which is often accessed by narrow stairwells. Made of three panels of glass, this transparent shower doesn't spoil the airiness of the space.

FACING PAGE The peaks and niches of an attic space are inherently interesting, so your attic-bath design can be simple. This space has been tiled from floor to the vaulted ceiling in creamy ceramic tile, making it possible to leave the shower open (it's hiding behind the simple vessel sink).

special considerations for attic baths

If you're lucky, your attic includes windows to let in the light and pull in a treetop view. If not, think about adding skylights or dormers in your attic renovation plans. Dormers have the advantage of offering a bit more headroom.

Attics can be hot in the summer and cold in the winter, so it's critical to work in the right ventilation and insulation. You also may need to consider adding a localized heating and cooling system in this peaked space.

FACING PAGE TOP The slender furniture-inspired vanity under a sloping wall makes efficient use of a vaulted ceiling.

FACING PAGE BOTTOM With their peaks and dormers, attics are inherently charming spaces. Make the best use of space by tucking the tub near a knee wall, being mindful of leaving 7 ft. of head clearance for entering and exiting the tub.

ABOVE Adding a dormer or a skylight to an attic bath buys the space more light and headroom. In this locker room–inspired attic bath, the skylight opens for ventilation or the whole stall can be sealed for steamy relaxation.

basement baths

●●● FINDING SPACE FOR A BATHROOM IN the basement is a more cost-efficient option than expanding the footprint of your house, but there are special considerations when putting a bath down under.

A concrete floor is an obvious challenge when installing plumbing lines. Most contractors recommend showers instead of tubs, especially if the shower can be tied into existing floor drains. An up-flushing toilet, which pumps water up to an overhead drainpipe, is another way to avoid busting through a concrete floor.

Basement bathrooms typically lack light. Battle the darkness with ample lighting, mirrors, and pale paint colors. These decorating tricks will also alleviate the cramped effect of a low ceiling—another common feature of a basement setting.

ABOVE Walkout basements with full windows are ideal locations for adding a new bath space. This lower-level guest bath is simple in design but includes a few feel-good luxuries such as stone tile and a hand sprayer.

FACING PAGE Rather than hide the rustic elements often found in the basement, embrace them. An old brick chimney serves as an earthy column in this bath. Its mottled color and texture inspired other stone surfaces and casual bronze fixtures.

More about...

TOP TIPS FOR ADDING A BASEMENT BATH

Check the condition of your basement. If walls are cracked or moldy, repairs need to be made before undertaking a remodeling project.

- Determine drainage. Dump a bucket of water down the drain closest to where you envision your bath. If the water drains quickly, you're in luck. If not, call a plumbing or drain expert.
- Locate the bathroom wisely. Plan for a corner location if possible to take advantage of two existing walls. Make sure the area is dry and offers good airflow.
- Talk to a plumber. Most plumbers will consult on a remodeling project for free or for a small fee. Many home remodelers save money by hiring out the plumbing work and doing the finish work.

room conversions

● ● ● IF YOUR HOME'S BED-TO-BATH RATIO doesn't work for your family's needs, consider taking space from a bedroom—or grabbing the whole room—for an extra bathroom. This is a less costly option than bumping out or adding on to your house. Consider how you can tap into existing lines by backing or stacking your plumbing to save additional dollars.

When converting an existing room to a new use, you will most likely need to get a building permit. Contractors typically handle this detail, but if you're doing the work yourself, you'll need to find out whether a permit for this type of remodeling is required in your area.

Also consider how the conversion will impact your home's resale potential. Check with a local realtor to learn if a three-bedroom, two-bath home, for example, has more buyer appeal than a four-bedroom, one-bathroom residence.

Converted bedrooms tend to be small and boxy. Break up the square lines by putting fixtures on a diagonal and adding large mirrors for extra dimension. A bronze chandelier tops this white marble bathroom with pretty style.

If you think you might need extra sleeping space in the future, design a converted room with bath fixtures in a small portion of the room so you can easily reclaim some space later. In this glam conversion, a clawfoot tub takes up no more space than a bureau, and the commode hides in the former closet behind it.

Open up the closet in a bedroom-turned-bath to allow for a dressing-room space. The graceful moldings on this freestanding tub blend beautifully with the room's substantial moldings, making it appear as if the bath was there all along.

finding your style

• • •

WOW! THERE IS A LOT OF STYLE IN THE BATH PRODUCTS AISLE. FOR some, that makes shopping for shiny fixtures and multicolored surfaces as thrilling as it is for a 5-year-old touring a toy store. For most, however, sorting out all the options and pulling together an eye-pleasing room design is a daunting process.

Of course, designing a bathroom is complicated by the fact that the overall investment is a substantial one. You'll be making decisions that you will be living with for a long time. And though creating a bathroom that appeals to you is a top priority, thinking about what the rest of the family wants—and even what potential homebuyers might like down the road—has to factor into the project.

So where do you start? First, take some cues from your home's architecture. Look around to determine which elements should stay consistent from room to room, such as moldings, a color palette, or overall architectural style. You don't have to match the rest of the house exactly, but whatever style, color, or materials you choose should complement the architecture and furnishings found elsewhere in the house.

With a candy store of colors and finishes available for the bathroom these days, it's easy to conjure up a design in your personal style. Pale glass tile, sculptural fixtures, and eye-catching folk art make an individual statement in this modern bathroom.

Spend time focusing on what looks you gravitate to. Flip through the pages of this book to check out current looks in bath design. Go through images in magazines and Web sites. Flag the rooms that grab you at first glance, without analyzing why you like them. Pull your family into the exercise to determine where your likes converge.

style that suits you

●●● MORE THAN ANY OTHER ROOM IN THE house, the bathroom is a multisensory space. When you plan the elements that you want in this room, don't just think about how it looks—consider how it feels as well. What surfaces do you want to walk on when your bare feet hit the deck in the morning? Do you want lighting and color that energize you in the morning or relax you at the end of the day . . . or both? Do you need a bath that accommodates a busy family or provides a cozy escape for you alone? Think about these questions as you design a room that satisfies both your eye and your heart.

ABOVE Colorful laminate cabinets and faux-wood laminate flooring create contemporary style on a budget. Laminate surfaces are also easy to clean and impervious to water—a good combo in the bathroom.

RIGHT Recycled wood and stone create a serene and natural scene in this powder room. The simple design links to a woodsy landscape just beyond the window.

FACING PAGE Reproduction fixtures and simple beadboard paneling steep a bathroom in cottage style. Beadboard is sold by the strip or in paneled sheets, making it an affordable surface option when sealed in paint formulated for bathrooms.

personal looks

●●● IT WASN'T LONG AGO THAT WE DECORATED by the book—or by the era—slavishly following foolproof design formulas or period-perfect interiors. Now, creating personal style is the overarching design trend. We want our homes to be an expression of our lives, our loves, ourselves.

Because eclectic design is more about mixing rather than matching, it's not the easiest trend to follow. One secret to success is to keep it simple. Cabinetry with clean, straight lines, for instance, will marry easily with a curvy clawfoot tub. When accessorizing, throw a surprise into the mix—such as pairing a mirror with a heavily carved frame next to super sleek lighting. When narrowing down your fixtures and finishing touches, think about items that have meaning to you, limiting yourself to a chosen few.

ABOVE The clean finishes and stripped-down forms typically found in the bathroom mix easily with many time periods and styles, making it simpler to combine styles. A carved gilt mirror and shiny stainless finishes blend seamlessly in a bath pared down to elegant essentials.

RIGHT Classic chrome and tile harken back to bathing spots of the past, but a glass shower door exhibits a taste for up-to-date materials. To create an eclectic look, fearlessly mix eras and use few, but quality materials.

Is it modern or a stripped-down version of country style? It doesn't matter when personal style is the goal. Tongue-and-groove cabinets and walls are rooted in cottage style but are clean enough to mix with sleek lighting and accessories.

classic romance

●●● YOU KNOW YOU'RE A DECORATING ROMANTIC when your rooms are dressed with lace and floral patterns. Or maybe you yearn for a grand old Victorian charmer, complete with ornate moldings and rich wood.

For another hint, think about how you shop. Do you prefer to duck into a vintage clothing shop rather than the latest designer hot spot? Classic romance can encompass many things.

While the romantic style is often considered a female preference, it doesn't mean you can't work it into a bathroom that a man will like. Classic, traditional styles include many features that both genders can enjoy, like carvings and curves. The keys are to add romantic touches in small doses and to keep the overall room light and airy.

To give this style a try, start with the basics: ornate fixtures, traditional surfaces such as marble and porcelain, patterned wall coverings or fabric, and carved woods. If you want more drama or romance, try an elegant chair with a floral pattern or a gilt mirror.

ABOVE Too much white can leave a space cold. In this master bath, soft blue solid-core countertops add a whisper of color to highlight the simple white cabinetry and chrome accents. A French chair and patterned towels add to the romance.

RIGHT Amp up the romance in a bathroom with pretty finishing touches. When set against a pale backdrop of graceful wallpaper, gauzy linen window shades, and white woods, a silk pendant lamp and ornately carved mirror are showstoppers.

For a classic look, rely on classic materials. Gleaming gold-veined marble sets the stage for a traditional pedestal tub. Glass-front cabinets and a touch of gilt add a layer of sparkle.

traditional elegance

●●● TRADITIONAL LOOKS HAVE MANY FACES. Even if you don't embrace the formality of a vintage Victorian home or the frills of a romantic setting, it does not mean that traditional style can't work for you.

If you're a formal person who likes balance and order, then a bathroom that is steeped in the classics could be perfect. Look for patterns that are crisp and symmetrical and for finishes that are polished rather than matte. Storage will be important to this character-rich, but neatly arranged design scheme.

ABOVE Navy and white is a classic color combination that seems tailor-made for the bath. For a crisp but less stark look than bright white, the scene is softened with creamy paint and linen fabric.

RIGHT Clean-lined walnut cabinetry conjures 1940s glamour. The dark wood contrasts dramatically with polished floors and porcelain.

FACING PAGE Rich, polished woods and substantial moldings are hallmarks of traditional style. Update a classic by mixing in clean white accents and limiting (or eliminating) heavy patterns.

RIGHT The Romans invented plumbing, so it seems fitting that a bath harkens back to that era for classical inspiration. This new enamel tub is molded into a traditional work of art and surrounded by other classic images and materials.

BELOW Warm colors mellow a white bath into a classic room. Wallpaper that looks like aged parchment picks up on gold gilt and burnished brass knobs. For a traditional touch of comfort, a piece of upholstery is added.

ABOVE Victorian-era houses are being decorated with a lighter touch these days. Stripped of heavy pattern and ornamentation, this elegant bathroom shows off its beautiful bones, including leaded-glass windows and a classic diamond-patterned floor.

LEFT A vanity styled like a classic piece of furniture will anchor a bathroom in tradition. A marble counter and heavily carved mirror top off the look, along with a delicate mosaic backsplash and trellis wallpaper.

country chic

● ● ● THERE ARE AS MANY VIEWPOINTS ON country style as there are homeowners who love the look. Considering country design has long been the favorite and most authentic American look, that's a lot of looks. The big umbrella of country runs the gamut from the fresh airiness of a beach cottage to the clean, Shaker-influenced style of the Northeast to the woodsy warmth of a mountain cabin.

Are you a little bit country? Would you prefer to wear linen and denim rather than velvet and silk? Is your idea of a Saturday adventure checking out the local flea market? What about your idea of a getaway—camping by a lake or dining in the city?

Casual, natural, linked to our past, and connected to nature, country interiors reflect the way many people want to live at home. Like all other design categories, this style has evolved with the times to reflect our more sophisticated and personal tastes.

RIGHT Sprinkle in just a few classics to give a modern bath country charm. The country-inspired ticking-stripe valance and milking stool stand out in an otherwise stark, white-tiled room.

FACING PAGE BOTTOM For an updated take on country style, keep the backdrop clean and furnishings to a minimum. Squared-off moldings and plantation shutters add architectural character but keep the spotlight on a few favorite primitives and a character-soaked vintage clawfoot tub.

LEFT New vessel sinks update the silhouette of farm basins past and fit easily into today's simpler country schemes. A vanity custom built of whitewashed and sealed pine is as simple as a workbench and just as functional.

RIGHT Great country style can be both simple and bold. Taking color cues from a vintage pedestal sink, new beadboard paneling is no shrinking violet. Ebony woods and a painted tub keep the color visually grounded.

• cottage charm

Fresh cottage decorating is country's plumper, friendlier cousin. Doused with garden-inspired fresh color and layered soft cushions and fabrics, cottage style sets a serene background for a comfortable, gracious life. Pretty but not precious, cottage style mixes in a lot of curves, not to mention a few ruffles, along with weathered finishes and garden motifs. Add a bit of cottage character to your bath to soften its hard edges and slick surfaces.

RIGHT Borrow the clean, charming elements of a seaside home for pure cottage style. Mellow teak surfaces, white beadboard paneling, and other simple elements mark this bath with light and airy style.

BELOW Reproduction pedestal pieces hark back to the 1930s and '40s heyday of cottage decorating, but their function is up to date. A glass-stall shower introduces modern efficiency but does not intrude upon the room's charm.

RIGHT Fluid lines and fun shapes bring out the happy mood of cottage style. A sunny dose of yellow and a vivid floor pattern keep the party going, without adding too much pattern. The solid-core counter is reminiscent of Bakelite®, a type of vintage plastic and favorite collectible.

Partially paneled walls, or wainscoting, are a trademark of cottage and country looks. For visual appeal, work in the design rule of threes: Take the paneling to either one-third of the wall height or two-thirds to avoid cutting the room in half.

•creative country

The country life is all about kicked-back, casual living…and so is country style. Have fun thinking of new ways to capture the relaxed and resourceful spirit of country by using vintage objects in new ways. An old door, for instance, might be the perfect partial wall to create privacy for the loo. Pull your favorite country items out of the cupboard and put them to work in the bathroom as storage. Buckets can hold rolled towels, and ironstone platters can corral jewelry or perfume bottles on the counter. Using old objects in new ways creates style that's both functional and fun.

ABOVE The washbasin has come a long way since the days of the pump house, but its charming spirit lives on. New vessel basins and reworked country cupboards allow for plenty of country creativity, especially with new pump-style faucets.

RIGHT Clever recycling looks great—and feels great, too. Rewired schoolhouse lighting and a gothic window turned mirror are sculptural art, especially when paired with an old farmhouse sink.

More about...
RENEWING AND RECYCLING

replacing the main elements in your bath—the sink, tub, and shower—are the big-ticket buys in a renovation. If your fixtures are in good working order and in tune with your style and your home's architecture, think about refinishing rather than replacing them. With replacement costs for a tub alone reaching into the thousands of dollars, refinishing is a far less expensive option.

Porcelain, fiberglass, and cast-iron fixtures are all candidates for resurfacing. It's a tricky process, and one best left to professionals for a smooth, successful surface. While you're upgrading a basin's finish, invest in new low-flow faucets and showerheads. These will save you money and update your look in one turn. One caveat here: If you need to remove the fixture to refinish it, you won't see this kind of savings.

If you don't have fixtures worth freshening, you can still recycle. Most cities have a Habitat for Humanity® ReStore®, which sells donated building and decorating materials of all types at drastically reduced prices (find the nearest one to you at www.habitat.org). From cabinets to windows to bathroom fixtures, you can reuse and recycle—and reduce your budget—by stopping here first to see if they have just what you need.

Is it country or is it modern? The best schemes have one foot in both styles. This bathroom borrows humble materials from country decorating, such as galvanized and stainless metals and pine planks. But the spare, sleek look of the stainless tub stamps it thoroughly modern.

RIGHT For a room rich with character but easy on the budget, remake vintage furniture into a bathing beauty. Once a dark, marble-topped bureau, this piece was fitted with an undermount sink and faucets and splashed with high-gloss white paint.

FAR RIGHT Even if you roll off the wrong side of the bed, a bathroom with a sunny attitude is a mood-changer. Golden yellow paint and bright white reproduction fixtures and subway tiles kick off the look; classic basketweave vinyl and marble tile add subtle texture.

Functional collections are a hallmark of resourceful country style. A trio of framed mirrors reflect clean and simple country style and bounce light around the small room. The vintage mirrors top new bureau-style vanities with galvanized counters.

The peaks and crannies of attics offer opportunities to think outside the box.
In this pass-through room with limited wall space, wall-mounted sinks under
a bank of windows go with the flow when mirrors are installed on the glass.

clean and modern

●●● MODERN DESIGN IS ALL ABOUT CLEAN lines and pared-down shapes. This sleek style statement moves easily into the bathroom, given the inherently simpler elements that go into the space. The advantages of a spare bathroom are obvious—less ornamentation means easier cleaning for you.

The challenge with this style of decorating is to keep the modern edge from becoming too stark and sterile. The most successful modern schemes are understated, warmed by simple textures, organic shapes, and subtle pattern. And, like other design looks today, they are less studied and more personal. Even if you have a more traditional approach to decorating in the rest of your home, a bathroom offers an opportunity to try a more modern aesthetic. Just pare down your design a bit to come up with your own take on modern. An object-free room in your home can become a refreshing retreat.

If you already know you are a true modernist who loves uncluttered environments where every item performs a function or who anxiously awaits the next slimmer, high-functioning electronic gadget, then there's no question modern style is for you.

LEFT Fluid lines act like a softening agent in spare modern bathrooms. A single, elongated "S" curve envelops a cloverleaf tub and walk-in shower—making an efficient use of space in the process. A slate countertop and tile in two sizes provide textural intrigue and a link to weathered bark outside of the windows.

BELOW Modern looks warm up with touches of wood and other contrasting materials. A wood floor adds warmth underfoot, grounding freestanding pieces such as the acrylic tub and laminate chest of drawers. An ebony acrylic sink offers its organic shape to the artful mix.

FACING PAGE FAR LEFT Symmetry is a central principle of modern design. Topped with etched blue, tempered glass, an apron-front shelf spans two walls in this bathroom. The side-by-side sinks, mirrors, and lighting fixtures keep the ledge in balance.

FACING PAGE LEFT Whether in the bedroom, living areas, or bathroom, modern design keeps a low profile. Horizontal graining on molding-free teak is both sleek and warm, a natural partner to unpolished stone tile floors. The stone reaches up the wall and onto the tub surround for calming design continuity.

what makes it modern?

Visit home improvement and discount centers today and you'll find interior designers lending their talents (and their names) to products available at all price levels, bringing contemporary, high-style design with them. From graphic shower curtains to elegant tile colors, these fashion-forward pieces blend seamlessly with the key elements in the bath, which are inherently modern. Keep the look crisp and clean by using more paint color than pattern, especially to highlight the architecture. And remember the modernist's mantra— less is more—keeping the scene serene by avoiding the visual clutter of too many objects.

ABOVE A tiny powder room is a good spot for showcasing modern style. A round sink that can be mounted in the corner is an instant space saver. A tall, slender mirror lends the sink more status, and it links to the stainless-steel sink skirt, which can be found for a song at a home improvement stores (look for stove backsplashes). Pendant lighting that dangles like delicate earrings adds a finishing touch.

LEFT Bathroom cabinetry inspired by furniture pieces from the bedroom brings a familiar and relaxed attitude to modern spaces. Here, a lyrical cutout mirror frame and simple baskets mellow the starker side of modern's personality.

LEFT Creamy limestone has the elegant look of marble, but with a more casual, natural feel. Sold in sheets and tile formats, limestone is readily available. It provides a soft frame for glass mosaic tile and a subtle contrast to the gray counter.

BELOW Sleek laminate storage and glass make a cool couple. These tempered glass panels have been etched to bottle-glass translucence to add visual weight to the mostly white scheme. A driftwood-gray tile floor bridges the two materials, continuing into the shower stall for a chic and easily accessible look.

ABOVE Organized doses of clear, saturated color mark a room modern. In grassy green, a panel door slides open without slicing a small bathroom in two. A stained cement floor and outdoor side tables keep the "industrial chic" look going.

TOP RIGHT Keep upper walls clear of heavy cabinetry and pattern for a low-slung modern look. Grids of earthy ceramic tile and dark wood vanities (stripped of ornamentation) create a warm, casual take on contemporary style. Gooseneck faucets and a bentwood chair throw in some welcome curves.

RIGHT As a general rule, oversize tiles are more modern in appearance than small, uniform squares. Mottled, honed stone in 12-in. × 24-in. rectangles creates the earthy, modern backdrop for maple vanities and a storage platform.

Recent advances in the engineering of tempered glass have cleared the way for frameless shower installations. These transparent shower booths pair with virtually any type of bathtub. Combine one with an egg-shaped, freestanding tub for a chic look that also offers flexible room arranging.

earthy elegance

● ● ● A GROWING AWARENESS OF EARTHLY matters has impacted the bathroom in both style and substance. Maybe it started back in 1994, when federal standards began requiring toilets, showerheads, and faucets to use less water. If you haven't updated your water fixtures since then, consider this: A new low-flow faucet costs just $20 but you can see up to $200 in water savings per year. Going green, especially in the resource-gobbling bathroom, is a win-win that helps our wallets and the world around us.

From a style standpoint, a fresh appreciation for natural materials and a more organic aesthetic plays out beautifully in the bath. From recycled glass tile backdrops to natural stone floors, eco-friendly bath products bring a purity of design to the room, perfect for those seeking a balance to the plastic and techno forces that are so much a part of the modern world.

You don't need to live in a log cabin to bring out a bath's more rustic side. Weave in a few textural, natural elements to counter the glossy elements of a bath space, and watch how the contrast brings out the best in both for a casual, but refined mix.

Various forms of grasscloth wall coverings have been adding touchable, natural texture to the walls of our abodes for centuries. Today, look for grasscloth wallpapers woven of sustainable sources and colored with water-based inks. This straw covering blends calmly with birch cabinets and stone tile.

ABOVE Being greener in the bathroom boils down to choosing products that are renewable, sustainable, and/or made locally. This bathroom gets high marks in style and sustainability thanks to bamboo cabinets and recycled glass tile. As a bonus, the oak medicine cabinet is a vintage piece.

LEFT Texture is more common than pattern in modern decorating. Create a cross-hatched design in a painted or plastered wall with a special tool or a notched dustpan or squeegee. Sleek, metal blinds and smoky quartz floor tile complete the stage for a chic simple bathroom.

• eco chic

The interest in ecology-conscious design is no longer considered a fad that will pass or a trend that will wane; it's a widespread design and cultural movement. Consumers are asking for it, and the home industry has responded, with an array of green options that fill the aisles of home stores. Whether you're in the market for surfaces, fixtures, construction materials, or cleansers, check out those labeled green friendly. Along the way, you may discover a new aesthetic that pleases your senses.

TOP Wood in a bathroom may seem like a bad idea at first glance, but properly sealed, wood is actually a durable, easy-to-clean surface. A wood veneer panel creates an artful outline for the lighter wood vanity in this closet-turned-vanity niche.

RIGHT When you're lucky enough to have a rustic space, resist the urge to go too far. The decorating magic is in the mix of styles. Against a knotty pine and stone backdrop, a freestanding tub, glittery chandelier, and luxurious flokati rug make an intriguing contrast.

More about...
ENERGY
EFFICIENCY

Conserving energy in the bath is good for the planet . . . and for your budget. Consider these ways to save.

• Switch to long-lasting compact fluorescents (CFL) or LED bulbs. Get rid of those energy-grabbing incandescent bulbs for good. Compact fluorescents produce the same amount of light as incandescent types with one-quarter of the electricity. And they can last for years.

• About 75 percent of the water consumed in the home is used in the bathroom. Install as many water-saving features as you can, including low-flow showerheads, faucet aerators, and toilets. Look into the discreet urinals that are now on the market.

• Smart window placement and coverings can save you energy and utility costs. One way to make existing windows more energy efficient is to dress them in layers, with more layers in the winter to retain heat and a sun-control (and privacy!) layer in the summer.

• Consider an on-demand water heater. Also, gas water heaters save more water than electric. If your water heater is warm to the touch, cover it with an insulator to avoid wasting energy.

A bath space doesn't have to be large to be luxurious. A small steam shower doesn't take long to wrap you in a blanket of warmth. Large squares of limestone framed by river stone mosaic tile underscore the natural sophistication of simple, clean-lined woods.

accessorizing the bath

● ● ● DON'T STOP DECORATING THE BATH before you add that final layer of trimmings and extras that express your personality and finish off the room's design. Collections, mementoes, art, and photographs— all of these items will layer meaning and interest onto what can be a stark space. Add natural objects for their inherent beauty. Seashells, sponges, and glass make a no-fail match for the bath because of their connection to water. To save yourself cleaning time, don't go overboard on accessories in this potentially messy, well-used room. And of course, stick to waterproof, moisture-resistant objects.

To make a functional space more personal and lively, mix in quirky elements. This seaside home features a bathing space that gets a kick out of kitschy sea-themed items. The mix works because the palette is limited mostly to turquoise, black, and white items.

TOP LEFT Mirrors and sconces are part of an accessories plan. Just as jewelry tops off an outfit, these dainty silver accent pieces add sparkle to a basic scheme.

TOP RIGHT Objects from nature make easy companions for stone and wood. Shapely glass apothecaries can be used to hold accessories or bath supplies, serving as functional art.

LEFT With the proper ventilation, a bath can be a safe display area for framed art. This mix of vintage and modern accessories works well thanks to shared shapes and the simplicity of the overall design.

artful arrangements

Sometimes the most important rule in accessorizing a room is to know when to quit. How do you know when enough is enough? When your things start fighting for attention so much that no single item is a standout. For a calming but still interesting scheme, don't crowd the space. Be sure to leave room for you—and your eyes—to rest.

To create an orderly, visually pleasing display, place the largest object first, then fill in around this focal-point piece, staggering heights as you go to create a grouping with depth. Play with your arrangement until it pleases your eye. As a general rule, one standout piece is better than a handful of mediocre ones. Finally, an odd number of objects (such as three or five) will create a more dynamic display than those that have an even number of items.

When arranging multiple items, start with the largest object first and build around it. Though there are many items on this wall, they are balanced on either side of the focal-point mirror. This organizes and calms the grouping, as does their similar materials.

More about...
TIPS FOR SUCCESSFUL ACCESSORIZING

use trays to group similar small items so that the display reads as one unit. This keeps objects orderly and more pleasing to the eye.

- Simplify your style in a small bathroom space by accessorizing with objects that are similar in style, color, or type. For eye-catching displays, mass the objects in one spot—a wall or shelf, for instance—for visual impact.

- Make a statement by using multiples of a single piece. A lineup of bold candles or a well-placed series of framed pieces creates design rhythm that calms the space by leading the eye easily around the room.

- Decorate with objects you love, especially in a personal space like a master bathroom. Start with a favorite piece, then select other accessories that complement or are inspired by the object.

- A sense of balance is important to a successful room scheme. Use symmetry in formal rooms by selecting twin items and placing them on either side of a focal point, such as a gorgeous tub. For less formality, create an asymmetrical display by balancing one large piece with two smaller ones.

TOP In bathrooms that are clean and serene, even subtle accessories become standouts. The Lucite® "ghost" chair offers a handy place to sit as well as a sculptural accent.

LEFT The best bath accessories are those that look pretty and perform a necessary function. A tub-side caddy can hold lotions, potions, and other pampering objects. Hung on simple hooks, even the towels make a style statement.

tubs, showers, sinks, and toilets

● ● ●

FURNISHING THE BATHROOM HAS TAKEN A DRAMATIC DESIGN TURN. Once stamped out in standard-order styles, tubs and sinks are now molded, pounded, and crafted into objects of art—like functional sculpture that pleases the eye while it gets the job done. The ultra-utilitarian showers and toilets of the past have gotten into the act, too, with sleeker forms and a whole lot more function.

Savvy, design-conscious consumers are spurring the change, demanding fixtures that are both chic and efficient, with affordable spa-inspired extras that improve your attitude and your health while going easy on the planet. Smaller but deeper soaking tubs let you unknot, chin-deep in warm, still water. Pared down to their essence, showers encased with pure glass can seal tight on demand, when your skin, sinuses, or muscles could use a resort-quality steam. Toilets with anti-bacterial surfaces practically clean up after themselves while using a fraction of the water their earlier counterparts did.

Artful, freestanding tubs have made a big splash in the bath-product market. This deep, egg-shaped soaking tub offers room-design flexibility; it can be placed to take advantage of a view.

With your budget as your guide (and ever-present taskmaster!) and the kind of pampering you want as your goal, consider the roundup of options for tricking out what's soon to be your favorite room in the house.

bathing beauties

●●● THE HISTORY OF THE BATH IS A FLUID ONE. IN ANCIENT cultures from Japan to Egypt, the bath was as much about spiritual purification as it was about a good scrubbing. Bathing as a ritual is woven through all religions, and bathing for relaxation (in public) can be traced back to the fifth century BCE. It's no wonder the tub is an alluring centerpiece in our modern lives.

The American bathtub story starts in 1883, four decades after the National Public Health Act passed a plumbing code for the United States that relied on cast-iron (rather than wood) water pipes. By 1883, Kohler® and the Standard Sanitary Manufacturing Company (now American Standard Brands®) were marketing cast-iron troughs with smooth, cleanable, enamel interior surfaces and four fancy legs that were pretty enough to go from the hog pen to the hearth.

The bathtub has traveled a long way, its evolution fueled by advances in materials, manufacturing, and consumer tastes. Today's bathing spots can be as high-tech, or as utterly simple, as you desire.

ABOVE Extra-deep soaking tubs are gaining popularity as a peaceful counter-balance to our plugged-in, overcharged lives. These tubs recall the quiet ritual of the Japanese bath.

RIGHT Built-in tubs can make a dramatic statement that reinforces the architectural style of your home. Centered under traditional, double-hung windows, this white-paneled oval tub is as classic and clean as the rest of the home.

CHOOSING A BATHTUB FINISH

there are far more tub finishes today than there were in the late 1800s. Which one you choose depends on a combination of style, comfort, ease of upkeep, and budget. This information will help you make the right choice for your needs.

Fiberglass: Also known as FRP, or fiberglass-reinforced plastic, a tub made from this material is formed by layers of fiberglass that are coated with gelcoat resin. The bathtubs are lightweight and have a repairable finish. On the downside, the tubs tend to flex and can crack. The finish tends to fade. Fiberglass is usually the least expensive option.

Porcelain: This classic material is still quite common and is another affordable option. Also called enameled steel, the tub is stamped from a thin sheet of steel then finished with a layer of porcelain enamel. The tubs are durable, easy to clean, and retain their glossy finishes against most chemicals. However, the surface can chip under impact, the shapes and sizes can be limited, and they are heavier than fiberglass or acrylic models.

Acrylic: This synthetic material lets manufacturers design and mold bathing units to their hearts' content. The units are made by using fiberglass sheets (for reinforcement) beneath vacuum-formed sheets of colored acrylic. The advantages are similar to those of fiberglass, though acrylics are more durable and more expensive. The range of shapes, sizes, and colors is impressive.

Cast iron: The availability of vintage clawfoot tubs indicates the durability of this material. Cast-iron tubs are made in the same way they were a century ago: Molten iron is poured into a mold and, when cool, is fused to a thick layer of porcelain enamel at high temperature. The finish is resistant to chipping and scratching. The look is luxurious, and the metal retains heat better than other materials. The tubs are extremely heavy, so extra labor and floor reinforcements are needed.

Solid surface: Solid-surface materials have been around since the 1960s but have only recently moved into bathtub applications. Pick your color or pattern (many mimic natural materials) and shape—there is no end to what this material can be designed into. The materials retain heat well, and are durable and easy to clean. However, the tubs can be heavy and are relatively expensive.

Cultured marble: These bathtubs are made from crushed limestone mixed with resin. The freestanding pieces are finished with gelcoat, which is more durable when bonded with marble than with fiberglass. This type of tub typically costs somewhere between the price tags found on acrylic and cast-iron tubs.

Stone and wood: These tubs definitely have that "wow" effect, but they also come with a steep price. Custom-order tubs are available in granite, marble, onyx, limestone, and other natural stone materials. You can also order a tub made of teak and other specialty woods. Besides the high cost of these bathing beauties, stone bathtubs require additional structural support. Both stone and wood basins demand a good deal of upkeep to retain their original finishes.

Polished marble floors and a chrome console sink are matched with an up-to-the-minute oval freestanding tub. A traditional bridge faucet links the sleek new acrylic tub with the classic side of the bath's personality.

Tub sizes are trending smaller these days, giving over floor space to larger showers, to more storage, or simply to a lighter, airier feel. This drop-in tub, with its sleek faucet, doesn't steal the show but blends into the woodsy scene.

• choosing a tub

Shopping for a bathtub these days is a bit like deciding which car to buy. You'll have to pick from a lot full of different shapes, colors, functions, and upgrades. To determine what works best for your family means trying on a few for size. Keeping within the parameters of your room and your budget, research different models that might work for you. Then head to the showroom floor and climb right in a few. (Not to worry, the sales people have seen it all before!) Check for depth, size, and placement of jets. Settle back and adjust yourself to other comfort features such as armrests and neck support. Try out all the options.

One word of caution: Don't get a bigger tub than you need. Tub sizes are trending smaller due to the need for water conservation and the pinch of rising energy costs. Plus, even the largest hot-water systems might run out of warmth before a super-sized tub is filled. No matter if your tub holds 50 gallons or 200, however, consider adding an inline heater to maintain a constant water temperature while you're bathing. For large tubs, you'll also need to check the manufacturer's specifications to determine whether you need to reinforce floor joists to handle the filled tub's weight.

LEFT Minimally designed surrounds can make drop-in tubs fit into clean, contemporary scenes. Solid-surface materials create a seamless look here, from tub to integral sinks. Exposed floor faucets break up the white with an industrial-chic presence.

BELOW With all the tub variations available, even small baths can be fitted with modern luxuries. The minimal deck space and corner placement of this jetted tub allows for a separate shower in this small master bath.

● freestanding bathtubs

It started with the iconic clawfoot model, but now freestanding tubs are being molded from a variety of materials into a gorgeous array of styles from elegantly traditional to sleekly modern. Because of limited standing space within it, a freestanding tub works best in a bathroom that has enough room for a separate shower stall.

There are some good reasons why you should try to work in one of these artful bathing beauties. The sculptural look of these units makes them instant focal points, adding drama to your bath. They have graceful lines and curves that will contrast the geometry of tiled walls and floors for more visual energy. Finally, the open space around—and sometimes under—the tub will make a small room look more open and airy than a built-in unit.

TOP Freestanding tubs are now offered at a range of prices, depending on the material used. Even so, these bathing beauties are an investment. Just as you "test-sit" a sofa before you decide, the best idea is to crawl into a showroom model to see how it fits.

RIGHT A variation of the clawfoot tub, the pedestal tub makes a focal-point statement in any bath. Its simple style fits as easily in a charming cottage bathroom as it does a spare, modern scheme.

ABOVE Enameled tubs that are partially built into the wall were standard order in American homes not so long ago. This deep, curvaceous soaker takes that concept to an elegant level, even as it harks back to Roman-era bathhouses.

LEFT Freestanding tubs boast ultra-simple designs that feel at home in most decorating styles. Pulled away from the walls, these glamorous baths have the practical benefit of preventing mold in a common hideout: where tub meets wall.

•built-in baths

The most common bathing basin in American homes is the built-in, or recessed, style. These tubs are built wall-to-wall into a niche, taking up only a slice of space. The exposed side of the tub can be coordinated to match other surfaces in the room, or it can come with an apron front that matches the style and color of the tub. Typical sizes are 30 in. to 34 in. wide, 14 in. to 20 in. deep, and 60 in. to 72 in. long. This type of tub is typically used as a tub/shower combination, and is a good choice for small bathrooms.

Another type of built-in tub is the platform model. These bathing wells have no apron front and are dropped into a platform or deck. Generally deeper than a recessed tub, this type works best in combination with a separate shower stall.

Corner tubs are made to tuck into a corner of the room. With either angled or curved fronts, corner tubs can counter the boxiness of a bathroom. They work best in large rectangular or square rooms.

TOP Recessed drop-in tubs can be easier to get in and out of, especially if there is an ample deck for balancing. The bottom of this self-rimming drop-in sits well below floor level. Plumbing is accessed from the basement.

RIGHT Corner tubs can be round, oval, or triangular. Extra surface space around the tub can conveniently hold both inspirational and practical items.

LEFT For a modern take on a drop-in tub, create simple surrounds with smooth-surface synthetics. This custom laminate enclosure is two-sided for a clean and compact look that doesn't require a second wall or niche for placement.

BELOW Built-in baths can be tucked into a walled niche, creating a cozy room-within-a-room feeling. Hushed, unpolished marble and barely-there spa colors keep the mood light and luxurious.

LEFT If a bathtub carved from solid stone seems a bit over the top, consider the forever nature of the piece. Heavier than a horse and carrying a $5,000 price, this classic limestone bath is built to stay put for a long, long time.

BELOW The multiple jets of a bath can be programmed to mimic the roll and rapids of a river. You get to select your sensation with the push of the button in this oversize tub designed for up to three people.

• specialty tubs

Custom baths and jetted hydrotherapy tubs can easily become more expensive than a living room full of furniture. But like a favorite sofa, a special tub can improve your daily life, physically and emotionally. After all, the health benefits of water therapy have been known for centuries. The Greeks and Romans discovered the healing powers of hydrotherapy way back when, and we still believe in the benefits of water for aching muscles and stressed-out minds.

Waterfall tubs. Exercise tubs. Tubs built for two. Soaking tubs. Bubbly tubs. At the high end, you can find all types of bathing experiences. Before investing, think about your needs now and 10 years down the road. The key is finding the model that not only looks right but also feels right for you and your family.

More about...
WATER- VS. AIR-JETTED BATHS

You have a choice between tubs that get their swirling waters from water jets or air jets. Here are a few pointers to help you decide which one.

Water experience: Water jets offer stronger, more targeted blasts for those who want muscles and joints to feel the power. Air jets provide a softer and quieter experience, more like a subtle, full-body massage.

Cleaning ease: Look for tubs that offer self-purging or flushing functions to keep the jets working at their peak. If you don't anticipate using the tub regularly, then air jets are the best choice because the blowers can be used to dry the jets out after use. Air baths are also less sensitive to bath oils and other additives.

Working parts: Water jets rely on an inline pump that recirculates a mixture of air and water to keep the water warm. Air baths inject water through a blower system.

ABOVE Resin tubs can be fitted with air jets that inject warm blasts of water through a blower system. Resin and acrylic tubs are typically priced between $2,000 and $3,000, so you can get the sleek good looks for less than those made with natural materials.

RIGHT Deep, European-style soaking tubs are artfully simple in design. They mix easily with classic or contemporary styles . . . or an eclectic mix of both, as this personal statement illustrates. Set a dramatic stage for a focal-point tub with a curtain that can be pulled closed for privacy.

bath faucets

Top off a bathing beauty with a
just-right faucet, just as you would top
off an outfit with the perfect jewelry.

RIGHT Install deck-mounted tub fixtures
on the corner that is the most accessible.
The fittings in this new built-in tub include a
handheld sprayer to add a shower function
and convenience.

BELOW A classic bridge fountain
reinforces the five-star quality of a classic
hotel-style bathroom. A handheld sprayer
and an extra-deep trough-style tub add
European sensibility to this simple space.

ABOVE New stripped-down floor-faucet systems are available for the modern freestanding tub. With hardware this clean and artful, who would ever want to hide it?

ABOVE Waterfall faucets and other clever tub fillers turn a standard bathing spot into a relaxing and romantic fountain. With strong individual pieces like this, you need fewer of them to create Zen-like simplicity.

RIGHT The utterly simple, straightforward approach of wall-mounted fixtures pairs well with pared-down, egg-shaped bathtubs. The tub is placed at an angle for easy access to the cross handles.

showers with style

●●● STATISTICS TELL US THAT MORE AMERICANS are shower people than tub people, mostly as a timesaving measure to help us keep up with our rushed lives. So it's no wonder that a separate, walk-in shower is at the top of a homeowner's remodeling wish list. In fact, some owners are eliminating the tub altogether in small or midsize bathrooms, making room for a larger, well-appointed shower. Not a bad idea, according to realtors—as long as there is a tub somewhere in the house.

There are other benefits to showering, too. Separate showers are easier to enter and exit, making it safer in general and especially for those with limited mobility. Showers are also easier to clean—no standing water and resulting tub rings. And showers can be outfitted with benches for seating, multiple shower heads, and steam functions that elevate a simple bathing experience to a daily spa treatment. Shower design has upped the bathroom's style ante, with enclosure options that include barely-there hinged glass, decorative glass, tiled partial walls, or even no enclosure at all.

An L-shaped shower and tub configuration fills a bathroom corner to make good use of space. This steam shower has a transom that can be closed to seal in the bone-warming, moist heat.

ABOVE Enclosed shower closets offer more privacy and the opportunity to trap some steam. Sealed with limestone and a single-panel glass door, this rain-shower area is easier to keep clean than an all-glass model.

TOP RIGHT The trend in shower design is leading toward spare glass stalls or no walls to leave the small space as open and inviting as possible. Without any steamy glass, walls, or curtains to block the window, this large shower becomes a room with a view.

RIGHT A tub/shower combination recessed into a two-wall niche has been the most common kind of shower spot in American homes. Now, you have more choice in tub types, such as this extra-deep soaker.

Framed shower stalls still have a place in today's bathrooms. This sliding glass door is custom-sized to the jetted tub. Note the squeegee hanging conveniently inside the shower, a necessity for keeping glass crystal clear.

Glass and stone combinations create a warm and modern statement. This open-door shower is created with three plain panes of tempered glass and a contrasting slate-tile wall. The tile turns the entire wall into a focal point and pulls together the scheme.

• shower surrounds

Shower walls and floors take a daily pounding from water and its humid vapors. That means what happens behind the scenes is of critical importance. Start with quality, water-resistant wall materials. There are many affordable materials that will last for years without deterioration. But regardless of the cost, the wrong materials or those that are poorly installed are bound to fail.

The two most common types of subwall are waterproof plasterboard, also called greenboard or tile backer board, and concrete substrate products such as Wonder Board® or Durock® cement backerboard. Although more expensive, concrete wall materials promise to last for decades no matter what the surface material. Plasterboard is not as durable, especially with tile installations that can

crack or crumble, leaving the subwall exposed to water's damaging effects.

Of course, the surface material itself must be waterproof (completely preventing water penetration), not just water-resistant (which resists but doesn't prevent water seepage). Manufacturers offer prefabricated surrounds and shower bases made of fiberglass, acrylic, vinyl, laminates, and solid-surface materials sold in panels. You can buy a readymade, multipiece shower surround kit that can be assembled on site. You can also buy a one-piece surround (typically molded of fiberglass, gelcoat, or acrylic), but you must measure carefully to make sure the product can fit through doorways, down hallways, and around tight corners or you won't even get it into your bathroom.

Marble and marble look-alikes are classic bathroom materials that can swing traditional or contemporary in style. Creating an oversize grid, these 10-in. tiles lean modern, especially when paired with smooth, clean glass.

More about...
SHOWER SURFACES

ℹ️ f a custom shower stall is in your plans, you have a choice of surface materials. Here are some pros and cons to consider.

SOLID SURFACE
Pros:
- A vast range of colors and patterns.
- Harder-than-stone durability.
- Fade/mildew resistance.
- Solid-surface shower kits are available precut into panels and finishing moldings and predrilled to go with standard fittings to make the project accessible to the experienced do-it-yourselfer.

Cons:
- Solid-surface materials can scratch.
- An experienced fabricator is critical for a custom solid-surface shower.
- Can be expensive, approaching the price of natural stone.

FIBERGLASS AND ACRYLIC
Pros:
- These synthetics are waterproof, durable, and simple to clean.
- You can find them at affordable price points.
- Available in all-in-one units if space allows (these are most often used in new construction) or in three- and five-sheet units in various sizes.

Cons:
- Considered a basic product that won't positively impact resale of your home.

CERAMIC, PORCELAIN, GLASS, AND NATURAL STONE TILE
Pros:
- Countless colors, grains, designs, and materials to create personal style.
- Waterproof, durable, and easy to maintain.
- If properly installed on concrete substrate, it will last for decades.

Cons:
- Grout can mildew and be difficult to clean, so look for mildew-resistant grout in gray or darker shades to make it look good longer.
- Natural stone products will need to be sealed and cleaned.

PREBONDED TILE
Pros:
- Easier to install than individual tiles.
- Available in mosaic style and pre-grouted sheets of 4-in.-square tile.

Cons:
- Small tiles mean more grout lines to seal and keep clean.

PLASTIC LAMINATE
Pros:
- This type of synthetic product resists scratches and abrasions better than fiberglass and acrylic.
- Can have a less molded or assembly-line appearance.

Cons:
- Still has a stock appearance and lacks personal style.

• super soakers

The shower is the new hot spot in home remodeling projects and new construction, thanks to all the new functions now available for the home bath. Many are available as add-ons or retrofits that won't bust the budget.

A handheld shower is one such option. It allows you to hold the blast of hot water just where you need it to ease your body's aches. Combine a handheld shower with a seating bench, and you've made your shower more accessible and safe. Hand sprays also make rinsing and cleaning the shower a breeze.

Body sprays mounted into the shower wall or on a shower tower will step up your bathing experience by increasing the amount of water coming at you. For the ultimate in relaxation, add four body sprays that are centered on the shower's plumbing wall, angled toward the center.

Ceiling-mounted showerheads or tiles, also called rain showers, release a relaxing spray of water that simulates a warm rain. Or, shop for a waterfall faucet that rushes at you like a mini cascade.

Shower jets deliver targeted blasts of warm water aimed at the back, shoulders, and legs. In this glass booth, the jets are aligned on the one solid wall for simpler plumbing. Overhead, a rain-shower head offers a gentler shower experience.

ABOVE Water tiles or rain tiles offer a gentle spray of water and can be installed in the wall or the ceiling for a multisensory shower event. This shower features the tiles on two walls along with a handheld sprayer in a stall that's big enough for two.

TOP RIGHT Multiple showerheads and jets can turn a shower into an everyday hydrotherapy treatment. Shop for luxury shower packages that offer a mix of components that are built into the wall, such as in this classic combination, or into an all-in-one shower tower.

Upgrade your shower experience simply by trading up from an old showerhead. This oversized model is designed to fit an extended arm, which centers it in the stall for a rain-shower sensation.

Handheld sprayers are popping up with new styles and functions. This modern number looks sleeker than earlier types and features a no-slip grip. Other models have massage functions and spray-intensity options.

LEFT What could be sleeker than an almost invisible glass booth of a shower? This one stretches from floor to ceiling to transform the ultra-spare shower into a steam shower.

BELOW The beauty of a shower made of glass panels is that it can assume many geometric shapes and sizes, and hinged transoms can turn any glass shower into a steam shower. Taking full advantage of its corner location, this small shower has room for a niche with a bench and a handheld shower.

•the steam shower

A steam shower is one of the most requested amenities in new bathrooms today. The health benefits of steam have long been touted in spas and health clubs. Now, bring the spa home for a daily dose of warm, moist air to release muscle tension, loosen joints, clear up skin and sinuses, and refresh both body and mind.

A steam shower is basically an enclosure with a vapor-tight door. You can relax in steam created by the shower, or add a steam shower generator. A seat or bench gives you a place to relax while you soak up the steam.

There are three basic options for a home steam shower: prefabricated, retrofit, or custom. Prefabricated steam showers are often made from acrylic and take up no more space than a standard prefab shower. If your existing shower is lined with tile, acrylic, or other nonporous surface, you can shop for a variety of prefabricated steam showers as well as conversion kits designed to transform an existing shower into a steamy sensation. The most expensive option is a custom-built shower that includes steam capabilities, or at least has the option of sealing the surround tightly.

You have to be careful when selecting surface materials for this type of shower so your house isn't also soaking up damaging steam. Nonporous tile, stone, or synthetics are the best materials to choose. Tile should be set in a mortar bed, not applied to water-resistant drywall or green board.

When a bathroom is outfitted with a jetted tub
and separate steam shower, you have your
very own spa. Carrara marble tiles and sheets
complete this simple but elegant scene.

• shower fixtures

Shower fixtures have evolved into hard-wearing, high-functioning, and good-looking accents for the bathroom. In fact, there are so many options that shopping angst is a real possibility. Make it easier on yourself by purchasing complementary tub, sink, and shower faucets that suit the style and finishes in your room. Polished chrome remains the hands-down favorite because of its bright clean look and ability to keep its shine with little maintenance. Other options include matte chrome, pewter, bronze, and china.

Whether your bath project involves a minor sprucing up or a major overhaul, consider the new showerheads on the market. Many save water and money while giving you a more satisfying soak. Learn more about water conservation by visiting the EPA's WaterSense® program at epa.gov/watersense. WaterSense labels products that have been deemed to be water efficient, similar to its sister program for appliance grading, ENERGY STAR®.

TOP A classic shower tower consists of a rain-bonnet showerhead and a handheld sprayer that can be mounted to slide.

RIGHT Rain-shower, or rain-bonnet, showerheads are large, often ceiling-mounted fixtures that produce the calming sensation of a warm, gentle rain. Today's models are more water-efficient than in years past.

Give your bathroom a finished look by coordinating metal finishes. Brushed stainless steel coats the fixtures, handles, and frame of this semi-enclosed shower for a pulled-together look.

outdoor showers

The combination of rushing water and fresh air is an intoxicating feeling. Enjoy that rich, resort-like luxury just outside your door by installing an outdoor shower. An al fresco dousing can be as simple or as complex as you want it to be. A hose, showerhead, and a little privacy are the essentials. Take it up a notch with a shower pad that drains efficiently, such as several inches of sand and pea gravel. Or go all out with a tile or cement base that is slanted for drainage or installed over a drain and piping.

For the ultimate in simple luxury, an on-demand water heater will warm your fresh-air soak and allow you to use the shower during cooler months. These energy-saving water heaters super-heat water as it is used so that no tanks of water need to be kept heated. Affordable, portable on-demand heaters—designed to be carried and hooked up to a garden hose when and where needed—are available at outdoor shops and discount centers. If you have a covered area, install a small heater for a more permanent setup.

Outdoor showers created with natural materials blend easily with their surroundings. Mortared river stone and flagstone are sealed against moisture for durability.

TOP LEFT All-weather tile used primarily for pool surfaces makes a colorful choice for an outdoor shower stall. Shower fittings are available with built-in circular shower rods, called shower rings.

ABOVE Tuck an outdoor shower next to a privacy wall or outdoor structure to minimize construction. This pavilion-style shower gets its privacy from panels of outdoor fabric. Lush plantings increase the resort feel of this backyard shower.

LEFT Any protected area that is situated near a water line is fair game for an open-air shower. This country shower is wedged between painted grain storage bins. A shower deck installed on an angle prevents water from standing.

sinks with style

●●● LIKE OTHER BATHROOM FIXTURES, SINKS have stepped up their style game. Trough sinks, infinity sinks, stone sinks, vessel sinks—you name the look and the material, and there's a sink to match.

Porcelain has long been the top choice for sinks because of its lustrous, hard-wearing finish. Sinks molded of enameled cast iron—especially those shaped into ever-popular pedestals—are another classic favorite. But these traditional options are moving over to make way for stone, solid surface, stainless steel, glass, and ceramic. Vessel sinks have also popped onto—and in some ways taken over—the scene, sitting proudly atop the counter as opposed to their more humble, undermounted cousins.

Consider what types of sink materials mix well with the other choices you've made for the bathroom. If you've settled on a glass shower stall, for instance, consider a glass vessel sink for design continuity. Your bathroom itself will help you narrow your choices further by defining how much storage and counter space you need. Finally, your current plumbing configuration will dictate how involved—and costly—installing a new sink will be.

ABOVE Popular vessel sinks that hark back to the bowl-and-pitcher concept are now showing up in countless shapes and materials. This low-profile sink looks like a modern interpretation of the hydrant and bucket. Vessel sinks often lack overflow drains, so don't walk away from a running faucet.

RIGHT Undermount sinks pair perfectly with stone or solid-surface countertops for a seamless look. Simple wall-mounted faucets go with the flow of this easy-to-clean, contemporary combination.

ABOVE Who could deny the clean and sculptural beauty of a pedestal sink? With separate hot- and cold-running faucets and extra surface space, this classic beauty has a practical side.

LEFT Wall-mounted sinks slip into small bathrooms without taking up precious floor space. This oval model features a lower panel that hides plumbing and unscrews when needed for repairs.

BASIN BASICS

Y ou'll face three basic decisions when you're out sink shopping.

Mount: Winnow your choice by deciding whether you want the storage capabilities of a vanity sink or the classic looks of a pedestal. For vanity styles, consider whether a vessel or an undermount sink would blend best with the style of your house. Undermount sinks, especially integral sinks in which the basin is molded into the countertop, are easier to clean than vessel varieties that have more cracks and crevices. Easy installation and customization make vessel sinks popular among do-it-yourselfers. Don't forget wall-mounted sinks for tight spaces.

Materials: Consider how much use your sink will get and how much cleaning time you want to devote to it before you settle on a surface type. Stainless sinks, downsized for the bathroom, supply affordable style and low maintenance. Porcelain and enamel basins are perennially popular because they stand up to hard wear and hang on to their glossy good looks. But don't walk by new and improved materials, such as tempered glass, that appear fragile but have proven more impervious to scratching and chipping than porcelain.

Fittings and faucets: Vanities are fitted with standard drill holes that allow you to choose from hundreds of faucet styles. Vessel sinks often require wall-mounted faucets that add construction costs to your project. No matter what type of basin you choose, make sure the faucet extends well into the sink and is properly proportioned to your sink size. To keep a sink splash free, the bowl's depth should be at least 12 in. unless it makes up for shallowness with perimeter size.

• vanity sinks

The advantages of a vanity sink are pretty obvious: handsome cabinetry that will stash your bath products, hide the business end of plumbing lines, and support counter space. Choose from built-in, freestanding, or wall-mounted varieties. If you like the custom good looks of built-ins, tie in a vanity to the architecture found in the rest of your home either by finish or style for design continuity. Freestanding consoles that mimic bureaus and other furniture pieces bring bedroom warmth into a cold bath space. When sink consoles are perched on legs or mounted on the wall, they create open areas under the unit and an airier style.

Vanities run the gamut from curvy country to clean-lined contemporary, making every style stop in between. This double wall-mounted vanity keeps the look clean and tidy with simple, squared-off sinks and faucets.

More about...
SINK OPTIONS

drop-in sinks can be framed or self-rimming. Framed sinks are the least expensive types, often found in older homes and apartments. The sink drops into the counter and is finished with a flat metal frame. Self-rimming, or surface-mounted, sinks are made with a lip that is oversized to the hole that holds the basin. These sinks can be installed into any type of counter.

Vessel sinks are the cool new kids on the block, but their design is based on the vintage bowl-and-pitcher concept. As the name suggests, this sink is simply a vessel that sits atop a counter surface. Like an object of art, the vessel can take on myriad shapes, colors, and styles. Vessel sinks pair with nonstandard faucets that are either wall- or deck-mounted.

Undermount sinks offer a cleaner look. These newer types of sinks pair with solid-surface or stone counters and, like the name implies, are mounted from the underside of the counter. If the sink and top are made from composite resin, then the basin can be manufactured to be integral with the countertop.

TOP Stock vanities allow you to pick from a variety of predrilled countertops and standard faucets for an affordable custom look. Amber-hued glass mosaic tile tops off this maple vanity and its limestone-like solid-surface counter.

LEFT Vanities designed with furniture characteristics warm up a bathroom and visually link it to adjoining bedrooms. This art deco–inspired bow-front vanity offers the perfect barrel niche for a round, undermount sink, but saves space elsewhere by flattening into slender wings on either side.

• vessel varieties

Vessel sinks have popped up in bathrooms and showrooms across the country. Why the popularity explosion? Vessel sinks get bonus points for their relative ease of installation (no carefully cutout holes for the sink to fit into, just a drain hole). And they come in a seemingly endless variety of shapes, styles, and materials so you can pick the just-right focal point for your room. If you tire of the basin that once bowled you over, swapping it out for a new model is fairly easy. Plus you get a smidgen more counter space with some of these top-mounted basins.

Before getting completely lured in by their novelty and good looks, consider the downside of a top-mounted sink. They present cracks and crevices where the basin meets countertop that can be tricky to clean around. Because of the exposed edges, basins are prone to chipping and breaking. Also, the typical vessel sink is secured at only one point, making it less stable than undercounter types. A square or recessed vessel sink—which sinks about halfway into the vanity—offers more security.

So choose your vessel wisely. A classic shape and durable material will ensure more longevity. And hesitant housekeepers might want to avoid clear glass basins, which demand almost constant cleaning.

White porcelain brings its cleanable, high-gloss character to the vessel sink category, where it mixes easily with modern and traditional styles.

Sinks carved from stone have an appeal that is both earthy and elegant. Powdery smooth limestone makes up walls, countertop, and sink in this simple and sophisticated bathroom. The limestone is set off with dark, clean-lined woods.

ABOVE Vessel sinks can sit on any sturdy surface, allowing you a wealth of creative options. More shelf than vanity, this wall-to-wall ledge holds ample-sized top-mounted basins. The apron hides the plumbing and holds a couple of handle-free drawers.

LEFT Almost any vintage bureau, sideboard, or dressing table can be re-imagined as a bathroom vanity thanks to vessel sinks. The bowl-like porcelain basin and classic farmhouse faucet look at home atop an Arts and Crafts sideboard with its built-in backsplash of tiles.

• pedestal, console, and wall-mounted sinks

A pedestal is a freestanding sink with a one-piece basin and countertop. It is an enduring favorite thanks to its charm and ability to squeeze into small bathrooms. Pedestal sinks come in both traditional and modern designs, bringing their focal-point status to all bath styles.

Console sinks (those designed with two or four legs and a bit more surface space) are another option in the classic category. Small wall-mounted units take up the least space of all, especially if you consider the corner units that slip into the tightest spots. Like vanities, many pedestal and freestanding sinks are now available in multiple heights, including the standard kitchen-counter height of 36 in., making them more comfortable to use.

LEFT Pedestal sinks come in a variety of sizes and styles. This modern silhouette spans a mere 18 in. to squeeze good design into a small slip of space. A hoop faucet is easy to operate.

BELOW Borrowing the dreamy elegance of the infinity-pool concept, this spare, wall-mounted sink and faucet duo join in a modern romance. Stainless rails play a supporting role, as do silvery glass mosaics and a slab of Carrara marble.

Wall-mounted faucets that put the plumbing behind closed walls make tidy companions for modern wall-mounted sinks. This shallow trough-style sink appears pared to its essence for a contemporary style.

Chrome legs and a marble top mark a console sink with vintage hotel style. This double console features wide-spread faucets and undermount sinks.

More about...
SINK MATERIALS

Ceramic: It's what you think of when you think of sinks. Vitreous china, a durable nonporous ceramic with a hard, gloss finish, is the original choice. Vitreous china is formed by firing clay at an intense heat in a process that fuses the glaze, making it impervious to water, bacteria, and almost any cleaner you apply to it. Ceramic sinks are among the least expensive.

Enameled metals: Sinks of porcelain on steel (POS) and enameled cast iron are highly durable. Porcelain on steel consists of a thin steel shell coated with a chemically bonded glazed clay. The finish is smooth and tough, making it similar to china sinks. The price is comparable as well. POS is less expensive but also less impact-resistant than enameled cast iron. Cast iron is fired at higher temperatures than POS and is also a step up in price. But cast iron has a superior finish with brighter colors and deeper gloss.

Stainless steel: Now more common in residential bathrooms, stainless-steel sinks are showy and tough. They won't chip, rust, or stain but can scratch. When shopping, look for 18- to 20-gauge steel (the lower the gauge, the thicker the metal) that has a chromium-nickel ratio of 18:10. The chromium adds muscle; the nickel mixes in corrosion resistance. A good undercoating minimizes the noise for bathroom use. Though usually smaller, stainless-steel lavs are pricier than stainless kitchen sinks.

Natural stone: Marble, granite, and other stones make stunning and earthy basins, especially for vessel sinks that parade on top of the counter. Granite is the strongest and hardest of the bunch, but inevitable chips are tough to repair. Marble and onyx need to be sealed—and resealed—to prevent staining. Natural stone sinks sit at the high end of the price range, costing in the thousands.

Manufactured stone: Cultured stone is molded from a mix of pigment, resins, and pulverized stone. It's used for integral sinks at a variety of prices. Concrete has also appeared in the bath as cast vessels and integral countertop designs. Denser than your standard driveway concrete, it can be finished with either a textured or a smooth, polished surface.

Solid surface: Sinks made from solid-surface polymers are another stone-like option. These materials have the ability to mimic all types of materials, even bright solids that resist fading. Scratches and stains can be buffed out of these durable synthetics, and they can be fabricated into one-piece countertops that are seamless and easy to clean.

Glass: Despite its fragile appearance, glass can be a durable bath mate. Most manufacturers use tempered glass that will crack but not shatter if struck by a hard object. (Think windshield glass.) Tempered glass should be at least ½ in. thick for use in frameless shower stalls, counters, or basins.

gallery

sink faucets

Pick a spout that lives happily
with your sink, both in style and finish.

Think of faucets as the jewelry of your bathroom
ensemble and select the style that tops your bathroom's
look with a little sparkle—but doesn't distract from the
overall impression. The crystal handles and dainty curved
neck of this wide-spread (two-handle) faucet add just
enough sparkle.

ABOVE The marriage of a sink and
a faucet can be beautiful if they share
a few traits in common. This square,
marble wall-mounted sink has a striking
elemental quality, which is shared by the
simple wall spout and single-lever faucet.

RIGHT Play up the structural beauty
of a square vessel sink with an equally
substantial faucet. The clean cross
handles and stately faucet have enough
scale and stature to get noticed.

LEFT Lever handles are classic in style and easier to operate for those with hand-strength issues. This traditional type includes a flared faucet and other fine details.

BELOW A faucet upgrade can take your sink from ordinary to extraordinary. This intriguingly slender model in polished chrome doesn't compete with the counter.

ABOVE Pump-inspired faucets are a good match for small sinks and make a strong style statement. Make sure the faucet you choose extends to the center of a small basin to avoid splashing.

clever commodes

●●● SURE, THE TOILET IS ONE OF THE MOST recognizable, ubiquitous pieces of equipment in your home, but you might be surprised at the variety available. You'll select from a range of looks, types, and functions. There are one- and two-piece toilets. The two-piece types—with separate tank and bowl—fit more easily through doorways and into tight spaces, but are tougher to clean. One-piece units come out of the box in a single piece and often sport a low, modern profile. Most toilets are made from ceramic or porcelain and acrylics or plastics. Industrial modern looks are bringing stainless-steel commodes into the home setting.

ABOVE Low-profile toilets take up less visual space in the bath, but don't skimp on comfort. The elongated bowl of this one-piece model offers an easy seat in a narrow wedge of space.

LEFT Commodes can be found in friendly shapes and plenty of seat sizes. This rounded version counters the straight-edged trough sink in this clever kids' bathroom.

ABOVE Wall-mounted toilets, like faucets and sinks, put most of their workings behind the wall—perfect for modern schemes. Because the tank can be raised higher, the gravity-dependent appliance works more efficiently.

LEFT For a pulled-together look, select your bath components from the same product line. The pretty moldings and squared off corners give this "throne" a finished look.

• trends in toilets

Today you can find comfort-height models, which raise the rim from the usual 14-in. height to as much as 18 in. off the ground (the standard chair seat height). Anti-bacterial surfaces, built-in bidets, and tankless toilets add to the function and fun of today's "throne." Tighter flush standards since 1994 have improved water usage as manufacturers compete to beat the 1.6 gallons per flush legal limit. Some models with dual-flush technology use a mere 0.8 gallons to clear liquid waste.

ABOVE Water-shortage issues promise to boil over within the next several years, which is sure to impact how many urinals go into American homes. Relatively affordable and discreet, urinals can make liquid waste vanish in under 1 gallon of water.

RIGHT Though a standard in European bathrooms, the bidet's popularity is only beginning to catch on in the U.S. market. Maybe the intriguing funnel shape of this modern version and its twin toilet (with dual flush!) will capture attention in this country.

ABOVE Slick, egg-shaped commodes are filling the need for modern silhouettes. Oval-shaped floor and wall models nest at the high end of the market, but the price will come down as the toilet follows other bath trends finding their way from Europe.

LEFT Though it has a high-end attitude (and the price to match), the stainless-steel loo has humble beginnings: as institutional plumbing found mostly in prisons. Honed into the sleekest of forms, this duo of steel is practical to maintain thanks to its durability and cleanability.

More about...
FLUSHING TECHNOLOGIES

t here are basically four types of flushing systems in use in the U.S.

Gravity: Shop for this system if you want a quiet flush or have low water pressure. In the gravity flush, the tank holds the water above the toilet, and the lever opens the flush valve to release the water from the tank. In the bowl, the water pressure creates a vacuum or siphon effect that draws the waste with it. Meanwhile, an automatic valve refills the tank.

Power- or pressure-assisted: In part due to the dissatisfaction with the power of gravity systems working under the 1.6-gallon guidelines, power-assisted flushes are available—and are particularly attractive to homeowners who are replacing a toilet but keeping old pipes. These systems use compressed air to force the waste down the trap. This type is considered best for families where the toilet sees some hard wear. One drawback of this toilet is a loud—some say startlingly so—flush. These models are also more expensive than gravity models. Manufacturers are beginning to fill the demand for quieter, more water-efficient pressure models.

Vacuum: This innovative system literally pulls the waste down from below the trap, resulting in a quiet and water-efficient flush. Look for models that promote the most flushing power; performance of these models is weaker than pressure-assisted flushing, though they come with similar price tags.

Dual-flush: This interactive toilet system allows you to choose between a 1.6-gallon flush (for solid waste) and a 0.8-gallon flush (for liquid matter). At the end of the day, these smart systems account for considerable water savings.

cabinetry and other storage

5

● ● ●

CABINETRY AND STORAGE ARE THE HARDWORKING BACKBONE OF A
bathroom. No matter what size space you have, planning for the right amount and
kind of storage will make the morning—and evening—routines run more smoothly.
Besides the performance of these elements, their look will have a big impact on
your bathroom design. Just think about how much visual space the cabinetry and
companion countertops grab up in a bath area. Clearly, giving yourself time to
research your options makes good sense.

Before you decide on components, give some thought to all of the items that
will be called into play in your family's bath. Think about how essentials can best be
kept organized and close at hand. From bath and hair care to
medicines to shaving and showering gels—the bathroom is
easily one of the most product-laden areas of the house, which
is challenging given its small stature.

In this chapter, we'll take a look at the many options you
have for cabinetry, countertops, and storage, including creative
storage options that will work in any space, from grand luxury
baths to pint-size powder rooms.

The best bathroom storage is good-looking and hardworking. This cabinet climbs the walls for optimum use of floor space. Its white finish and open shelves at the bottom prevent it from weighing down the room's airy cottage feel.

cabinetry

● ● ● THE MOST IMPORTANT ROLE CABINETRY plays in the bathroom is pretty obvious—providing a stash-all. But the style and finish of these storage pieces also play a big part in the style direction your overall room takes. For instance, select polished woods to enhance traditional schemes, sleek modern laminates for a modern mood, or weathered woods for a rustic country statement. Though you don't want to make a radical departure from the rest of the styles and finishes in your house, the look of the cabinetry you choose in the bathroom is an opportunity to shift to a fresher style, or one that more closely appeals to your aesthetic.

Working enough storage into limited bathroom space is like putting together a puzzle. Everything needs to fit together, and there are a lot of pieces to choose from. Vanities run the gamut from undersink varieties to ceiling-high linen cupboards. Fittings can go behind doors and inside drawers. Storage can be fitted with drawers, shelves, tilt-out hampers, wire baskets, or cubbies for small items. You can even trick out your cabinets with warming inserts for towels or create tub-side storage that has a space for a small flat-screen TV to maximize fun and function.

Modern laminate storage keeps clutter corralled in a clean, tidy package.
Perched on square, stainless-steel legs, this vanity allows light to shine into
the far reaches and lighten the room.

ABOVE If your house leans traditional but you want a lighter, brighter look for the bath, consider classic marble and white cabinets that have traditional lines, such as doors with recessed panels.

TOP RIGHT For an efficient bath space, include multiple types of storage. Vanity drawers organize a jumble of grooming products, while stacks of towels fit neatly behind cupboards.

RIGHT Use the warm wood grains of cabinetry to balance polished finishes elsewhere in the bath. A wall of maple, built-in closets adds storage and stature to this combination gentleman's dressing room and water closet.

the elements of a quality cabinet

The old adage "Buy the best you can afford" holds true when it comes to bathroom cabinetry. Many manufacturers offer two or three grades of quality. One good indicator of overall durability is certification by the Kitchen Cabinet Manufacturers Association, which has rigorous testing on structural integrity, shelf strength, hardware durability, and finish quality. In a room that sees daily use and lots of splashing, the level of quality you purchase will determine how soon you'll be planning your next bathroom redo.

More about...
WHAT MAKES A QUALITY CABINET

Once you've arrived at a few styles of cabinets you like, check the manufacturer's specifications sheet against this list.

The cabinet box makes up the body of the cabinet and gives it structural integrity. In framed cabinets, the traditional type of construction, the frame is made of ¾-in.-thick solid-wood rails and stiles. Hinges attach to these face frames and are typically visible with the doors shut. Frameless cabinets have no face frames in front, so the doors attach directly to the inside face of the cabinet sides with cup hinges. Doors and drawers fit tightly with no frame, and often no hinges, revealed.

Doors made of solid-wood frames surrounding solid-wood or plywood paneling are your best bet. Medium-density fiberboard (MDF) is a good option, but the best cabinet doors are made of ½-in. to ⅝-in. plywood. The facings on better cabinets are most often made with high-pressure laminate or real wood veneer. Medium-pressure laminate over particleboard is the most affordable of the options.

Shelves in cabinets range from ½-in. particleboard, which might bow under the weight of heavy objects, to ¾-in. plywood. Plywood is the strongest shelving material, followed by MDF, then particleboard.

Drawers get a lot of abuse. High-quality drawers typically have solid hardwood or poplar sides and backs, with ¼-in. plywood bottoms glued into dadoes. In the best cabinets, drawer sides are dovetailed or doweled to the front and back, with a separate drawer front that is screwed to the drawer box for added durability. For a trustworthy drawer, look for sides made with ½-in. or thicker plywood or melamine stock doweled together. Lower-end cabinets feature drawer sides made of particleboard or MDF wrapped in vinyl and stapled and glued together.

Drawer slides should be heavy-duty, epoxy-coated components with ball-bearing rollers that operate smoothly and silently. The best setup is full-extension slides rated for 110 lb. Undermount slides support the drawer while staying out of sight; side-mounted slides that wrap around the drawer bottom also provide good support.

Hinges should be smooth to operate, easy to adjust, and sized to the door. Concealed cup hinges can be adjusted in three directions for easier door alignment and adjustment.

FACING PAGE TOP Drawer glides and stops help make drawers operate smoothly and safely. This towel drawer has an extra luxurious feature: a warming inset with a timer so your towels will be toasty when you want them.

FACING PAGE BOTTOM Substantial moldings, well-fitting drawers, and extras such as toe recesses all signify quality cabinets. This double vanity is back-saver height—at 35 in. instead of the standard 31 in., it means less bending.

RIGHT Peek at the cabinet's joinery to help determine its level of quality. Dovetail joints, which fit together like a puzzle, are superior to stapled or butt-end drawers.

Cabinetry can be designed with extra safety and function in mind. The slightly recessed base of this vanity allows for a strip of lighting that highlights the piece's dimensions and becomes a subtle nightlight.

Furniture-inspired vanities usher in fresh style to the bath. With chrome cup pulls and extra-wide drawers, this pretty white vanity has the charm of a vintage bureau—perfect to underscore the cottage style in this bath.

In a powder room that opens into the public areas of a house, select cabinetry that relates to your architecture for design continuity. Mission-style detailing and dark woods don't fight the feeling of this 1920s bungalow.

Drawer pulls and cupboard handles add sparkle to a bathroom. These circle pulls draw the eye, giving the piece architectural appeal and a dressy finishing touch.

Even simple cabinet styles can be the standout item in a bathroom. This golden, wall-mounted vanity contrasts with the mottled blue grays of slate tile.

Shop at home improvement stores, specialty shops, and online for stock bathroom cabinetry that boasts multiple components. This collection includes a freestanding armoire and a sink ledge that allows for universal access.

• types of cabinetry

The first thing you'll have to decide is whether to choose custom, semi-custom, or stock cabinets. Let the budget be your guide; but let your style decide. There are design-forward options at all price ranges.

Custom cabinets are at the high end of the price spectrum, but you can dictate the style, finish, and size. Local cabinet shops are often the source for custom cabinets, along with the many talented carpenters and cabinetmakers that work on their own. If you are working with a contractor, be sure to check the portfolio and references of the cabinetmaker in line to do the job. This is an area that requires skill.

Stock cabinetry, like the many other elements you will choose for your project, comes in many styles and finishes. You can find "off-the-rack" cabinetry on hand at home improvement centers and kitchen and bath showrooms. These cabinets are manufactured using standard shapes and dimensions, and often can be purchased and installed the same day. The price range of ready-to-wear cabinets is wide, with many well-designed options at affordable prices.

You might also aim somewhere in the middle between custom and stock cabinets and check out semi-custom models. In the most basic terms, semi-custom indicates stock cabinetry that offers made-to-order custom options. Better mid-priced cabinets use solid-wood frame construction. Pick your materials and finishes, door style, moldings and trims, and inner-workings of drawers and cupboards.

When you're in the market for stock or semi-custom cabinetry, measure the area you've reserved for storage and keep those measurements close at hand as you shop.

ABOVE Semi-custom cabinetry allows a homeowner to pick components to make the most of a space. An arched alcove, recessed lighting, and corner cupboards lend this wall a built-in look.

TOP RIGHT Custom cabinets (and some off-the-shelf models) allow you to mix woods for an interior that looks more evolved and personal. Slender, floor-to-ceiling cabinets pack in more storage without gobbling floor space.

RIGHT Customize any cabinet—even store-bought—with eye-catching knobs and pulls. This one is painted a soft sage green to pick up the shower's tile accent. A sconce mounted on the mirror ups the sparkle quotient.

cabinet door styles

Manufacturers make the same style doors and drawers at various price points. The price is driven by the material, hardware, and assembly technique. Though a bathroom offers a chance to take your style in a more modern direction, your bath will flow better with the rest of your interior if the style of the cabinets relates well with the architecture of adjoining rooms and the house in general.

The common door styles on the facing page—and the numerous variations of them shown in the photographs throughout this book— are available in both frameless and face-frame cabinets.

TOP For casual decorating schemes, cabinets with square recessed-panel facings add dimension and interest without a lot of ornamentation. Iron pulls that look hand-wrought match the heft of dark wood drawers and doors.

RIGHT Modern vanities often feature frameless cabinetry, where "slab"-style doors butt tightly together and the cabinet frame is hidden behind closed doors. Sitting on sleek, stainless-steel stovepipe legs, this mid-century modern vanity has flat doors that show off its artful wood grain.

gallery

door styles

Raised panel

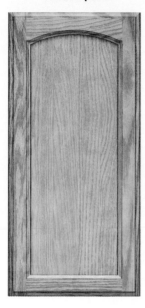

Recessed panel

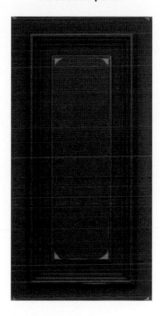

Slab veneer

Beaded solid

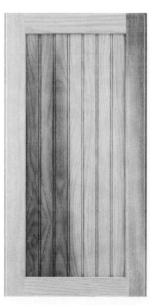

Beaded veneer

Square recessed

innovative
storage

●●● DON'T LIMIT YOUR STASHES TO THE KIND behind closed doors. Clever homeowners and designers have found ways to increase stowing power with baskets, well-outfitted medicine chests, open shelving, and niches.

Even a row of Shaker pegs or artful hooks can hold essentials, especially if floor space is limited.

Some homeowners and designers are including new, vintage, or unfinished furniture into bathrooms for a more personalized style expression. For the do-it-yourselfer, converting a bureau or a chest into a working vanity is a relatively easy project, especially if you choose a freestanding vessel sink and wall-mounted plumbing fixtures. Or, for a readymade option, look for the many manufactured options in freestanding vanities that look like furniture at first glance, such as a traditional bow-front dresser or a clean Parsons-style table.

Antique armoires and chests add both character and a cache for storage. This vintage pie safe has ample stowing power and a screened front to keep items within sight.

ABOVE Open shelves keep towels and necessary items in sight, perfect for a guest bath. Woven baskets store everything from bath products to plug-in hair appliances.

TOP LEFT Busy bathrooms can have the energy of a locker room . . . so why not borrow some cool fittings from the real thing? This white laminate partial wall offers a cushioned bench for dressing or drying and a series of cupboards for stowing.

LEFT Think of storage as an opportunity to get creative with modern storage components. Perfect for a small bath, these wall-mounted storage pieces have niches sized for towels and shallow drawers to keep cosmetics and jewelry within reach.

Even a trim bookshelf or étagère has a useful amount of storage. This rattan piece brings a relaxing, resort feel to this simple but elegant bathroom. It pairs with an antique chair to warm up the marble and glossy white space.

FAR LEFT Bookcase-style shelving built into the shower wall keeps little bath luxuries well within reach. Be sure to include favorite items that bring you peace, from candles to snapshots, to promote a relaxing bath.

LEFT For a personal touch, consider converting a favorite table or bureau into a vanity. A vintage table does the job in this powder room. A stretch of pretty linen hung by a simple tension rod adds softness and hides plumbing and supplies.

BELOW Think ahead if you're creating a bathroom from the ground up. This extra-deep (and tall) medicine chest features sliding drawer inserts for easy access to small items.

Have your classic pedestal sink—and storage too—by bringing in a vintage bureau as a clever dressing table. This piece has ample drawer space to hold towels and plenty of other essentials.

countertops

●●● REGARDLESS OF THE AMOUNT OF SPACE in your bathroom, countertops play an important role in your room's design. Like the cabinetry you choose, countertops make a style statement, one that you're not likely to change very often. Consider materials that are neutral in color and limited in pattern so you won't tire of the design as quickly and can freshen it with a change in paint color or accessories.

The counter's main job is to stand up against moisture. When choosing the look you like, consider the surface's resistance to stains, heat (as from a hair dryer), chipping, and wear. There is a wealth of materials that meet the bathroom's requirements, including natural and synthetic surfacing products available in a broad range of colors, textures, and price ranges. For the most part, your budget and cleaning preferences will narrow the choice for you.

Solid-surface counters can be purchased prefabricated to be sink and faucet ready. Undermount sinks are excellent companions for these synthetic countertops, which mimic creamy limestone.

A vessel sink molded from pure white porcelain will look at home on most any countertop and can save you money as well. A slab of limestone or other natural stone will be less expensive than purchasing a precut piece.

ABOVE Precut, solid-surface counters often come with a prefabricated sink basin. This pure white sink is easier to keep clean thanks to the seamless basin.

LEFT Marble slabs can be custom cut to fit your space. This piece was cut at an angle to make room for maneuvering in this narrow attic bath.

•natural
materials

Your earth-based choices include stone, tile, wood, glass, and concrete. Stone stands on the top of the price pedestal, but it can be cut into one of the most elegant, durable, nonporous surfaces out there. With the proper sealing and maintenance, it will last a lifetime. To get the look for less, use stone on a small vanity, or shop for stone tiles rather than cut stone to top your cabinetry.

Tile is a design dream. It's offered in a virtually endless spectrum of materials, sizes, prices, colors, and patterns. You can conjure up a watery spa scheme with recycled glass tiles or add pops of color with hand-painted ceramic pieces. Mix and match tile collections to personalize a bath with an artfully original backdrop. For a countertop application, choose a large format tile to minimize grout lines (though grout is stronger and more stain-resistant than in years past).

TOP Carrara marble is the superstar of surfaces. Its white base and subtle graining allow it to slip into many bathroom styles. Even a small piece of marble establishes elegance in this guest bath.

RIGHT Granite is the symbol of strength and earth-mined beauty. This black granite countertop matches the austere mood of a bathroom that features clean lines and natural materials.

Glass is becoming a
prominent material in the
bathroom. This tempered-
glass counter is elevated
slightly to get the most of
its shiny qualities. Let the
buyer beware, however—
glass demands regular
wiping and dusting.

•more natural choices

Wood, when properly sealed against moisture, can be a warm and workable surface for bathrooms. Think about the types of wood used on boats to get a list of best bets, which include teak, marine-grade plywood, and cedar. With interest in ecological home materials continuing to rise, renewable choices such as paper and bamboo have surfaced in the marketplace. Look for surfaces made from bamboo, recycled paper, or wood fibers that are compressed and held together with VOC-free, water-based resin for the greenest option.

The popularity of concrete as a counter material waxes and wanes, but because it can be cast into any shape and takes colored pigment well, it continues to be an intriguing choice, especially in contemporary interiors. Whether or not you choose it depends largely on whether there's a good fabricator in your area—unless of course you're handy with a trowel.

TOP Properly sealed wood is water worthy, as evidenced by the decks of many sailing vessels. This polished teak wood breaks up white walls and cabinetry to give the room definition.

ABOVE Countertops can set the style of a bathroom. To match the earthy, modern style of gray-stained woods, this counter—along with the floor and tub surround—was created with poured cement smoothed to a mellow sheen.

LEFT Metals are popping up as a modern alternative for counter dressings. Clad in a thin layer of stainless steel, this shelf-style counter is sleek and contemporary, especially when married to a stainless-steel basin and clean-lined faucets.

More about...
PROS AND CONS OF THE NATURALS

GRANITE

Pros:

• Granite countertops are a value-add for any home.

• It's nonporous, won't scratch or stain, and lasts forever when properly sealed.

• A honed granite surface is less porous than glossy finishes, but all granite should be sealed annually to keep it looking its best.

Cons:

• This is one of the most expensive counter options. For a less expensive option, look into granite tiles suitable for counter installation.

• It can chip or break from a sharp blow.

• Seams can be visible and require upkeep.

TILE

Pros:

• Glazed tiles stand up to water, stains, and heat.

• No other material matches the variety of designs available.

• Tile can be repaired.

Cons:

• Tile creates an uneven surface with grout lines that collect grime.

• Tile can chip or crack.

• It needs to be sealed according to the manufacturer's directions.

• Installation is moderately difficult for the do-it-yourselfer.

LIMESTONE

Pros:

• This soft, virtually vein- and grain-free stone has a clean but natural appeal.

• Limestone is more widely available, and therefore less expensive, than granite or marble.

Cons:

• This surface is a more porous type of stone, leaving it open to chipping and staining. Choose polished limestone to improve its armor.

• It requires both regular cleaning and sealing.

MARBLE

Pros:

• Marble has an understated, timeless elegance.

• Each piece of this crystallized limestone has its own veining and coloration.

• Marble is water and heat resistant and lasts forever.

• Tile applications have made marble affordable to a broader range of homeowners.

Cons:

• Marble is softer than granite, making it susceptible to stains, scratches, and chips.

• It's best to use cleaning products made for marble and to reseal the stone periodically.

CONCRETE

Pros:

• Concrete is a flexible and funky choice for bathroom counters.

• It can be tinted or textured into an individual style statement.

Cons:

• Concrete requires a professional fabricator or skilled do-it-yourselfer for polished results.

• Concrete has a tendency to produce hairline cracks.

• It's a porous material, so is prone to staining and burning.

SOAPSTONE

Pros:

• It resists stains, heat, and moisture.

• Look for soapstone with a high quartz content for a harder countertop.

• This material is available in multiple grades and prices.

Cons:

• Unless you're content with a worn patina, be ready to coat your soapstone counter with mineral oil regularly (twice a month in bathrooms that see average use).

• Soapstone can scratch.

• synthetic options

Synthetic surfaces include laminates, solid-surface materials (DuPont®'s Corian® is the best-known brand but there are others), and stone composites. The most affordable counter surface, by a considerable margin, is laminate. But that won't make your selection process any easier because there are hundreds of colors, patterns, and natural look-alikes from which to choose.

Solid-surface materials are generally cast of acrylic or an acrylic-polyester mix, and can be fabricated on site almost like wood. These products are also available in a mind-boggling spectrum of colors and designs. Many approach the look of real stone. The great advantage of solid surface is the seamlessness for easy cleaning—some even come as a one-piece counter with a basin molded in.

Stone composites have gained popularity because they have the look of stone at less cost. The composites, also called quartz or engineered stone, include a small amount of acrylic resin or epoxy for increased scratch and stain resistance. Some composites enjoy the eco-friendly advantage of having recycled glass worked into the mix.

TOP RIGHT Solid-surface counters can be rounded at the edges for a finished look.

RIGHT Solid-surface counters are available with the sinks molded within the counter to form one single piece. Without seams, the look is clean and simple—and stays that way with little attention.

Laminate counters can be bright and modern or subtle and natural. This counter option is paired with top-mounted sinks that are held in place by a metal rim.

PROS AND CONS OF THE SYNTHETICS

LAMINATES

Pros:

- Laminate is affordable, available in a vast spectrum of colors and patterns (including fool-the-eye twins to stone, wood, and other naturals), and relatively easy to install.
- The highest-end laminates offer cutting-edge printing and embossing processes.
- Laminates are impervious to stains and water. They're more resistant to heat than in the past.
- Some laminates contain recycled material and meet standards for low emissions.

Cons:

- The seams are often visible and can breach, letting water seep in and warp the material.
- Laminate can easily scratch, which typically means a new counter, since scratches can't be fixed. Textured finishes are better than flat ones at hiding imperfections.

ENGINEERED STONE

Pros:

- Also known as quartz, engineered-stone counters come in subtle styles that look like stone or in eye-popping colors.
- It won't chip, scratch, burn, or let in a drop of water.

Cons:

- Though engineered stone holds up as well as granite in most situations, quartz counters have less impact resistance and can chip around the edges.

SOLID SURFACE

Pros:

- Made of polyester or acrylic resins pressed with natural mineral materials, solid-surface counters boast clear, fresh colors and are able to mimic marble, limestone, soapstone, and other naturals.
- It can be molded to include an integrated sink, or is a perfect companion to an undermount basin.
- This material is water, heat, and impact resistant.
- Scratches and nicks can be buffed out.

Cons:

- The cost of some solid-core materials can rival granite and stone, but solid surface doesn't have the same scratch resistance.
- Prolonged heat can cause discoloration.

PAPER COMPOSITE

Pros:

- Made when recycled paper and wood is ground to a pulp and then compressed and saturated with low-VOC, water-based resin, this material is an affordable, durable, and environmentally conscious countertop option.

Cons:

- Paper-based countertops using phenolic resins are caramel in color, which limits (and dulls) the range of colors available.
- Some resins can darken with light exposure.

caring for
your counter

With so many counter options and—for most busy homeowners—so little time to choose, one way to narrow your choice is by the amount of maintenance you're willing to dedicate to the material. If your bathroom sees heavy use and your housekeeping time is limited, steer toward hard-wearing engineered products. If you want a high-style look in a limited space, stone might be your first choice. Whichever surface you choose, make sure you're willing to do what it takes to keep the material looking its showroom best.

LEFT Trough-style sinks look fresh and fun in today's baths. Usually made of porcelain or solid-core materials, these seamless sinks are easy to clean but gobble up counter space.

ABOVE Granite is the toughest of the stone options, but it needs to be sealed to retain its high shine. This polished granite counter has an earthy elegance that mixes easily with an unpolished tile backsplash.

FACING PAGE TOP Undermount sinks eliminate the banding required to hold top-mounted sinks in place. This also eliminates a visible seam that inevitably traps grime.

FACING PAGE BOTTOM Marble counters have one drawback: They tend to stain and can scorch. Use trays or baskets to corral bath items that might leave a ring or mark.

matching faucets to counters

● ● ● BEFORE MAKING YOUR FINAL DECISION on a countertop, think about what type of faucet you want to punctuate the design. These elements should be considered as a unit. Counters that have been predrilled to accept certain faucet styles will dictate your choice.

The style and finish of the faucet should relate to the counter material for a finished look. Pairing an elaborate, traditional-looking faucet with a bright solid-surface counter, for instance, might be visually jarring and spoil the professional, pulled-together look you're after. Likewise, topping elegant marble with a cheap faucet can downgrade the final design.

Faucets add a lot to a countertop: height, sculpture, and sparkle. Gooseneck-style faucets are finding their way into the modern bath, adding utility (no need to reach far down into the sink) and graceful lines.

TOP Wall-mounted faucets allow only the pretty parts to show, hiding water lines behind the wall. A pearlized solid-surface counter and glass mosaic wall tiles match the pure elegance of this pared-down faucet set.

ABOVE A single-lever faucet takes up less space and requires less cleaning than traditional countertop-mounted faucets. Squared off and clad in chrome, this unilever model has stature without marring the clean, sleek look.

LEFT Many sinks and counters come with holes drilled for a certain kind of faucet. In this case, a wide-spread faucet, with two separate handles flanking the spout, fills the bill. Its polished-chrome finish attracts attention.

RIGHT A single-lever faucet is easier to operate for those with strength or arthritis issues. This stainless model also offers a clean profile.

FAR RIGHT Faucets come in all styles and at all price points, but it's best to match a quality faucet with a quality counter material. Looking like classic silver jewelry, these elegant fittings complement a marble counter and backsplash.

Relatively new to the mainstream marketplace, wall-mounted faucets help you keep your counter clean. This modern unit includes a back plate for easier installation.

TOP Polished chrome has long been the most popular finish for faucets. Molded into classic shapes, this wide-spread faucet is stately enough for its marble counter companion.

ABOVE Brushed-chrome faucets have a more casual appearance. This set includes a soap dispenser to streamline cleanup.

Tall, arching gooseneck faucets make ideal partners for vessel sinks and large basins. The faucet reaches to the center of the basin for minimal counter splash.

selecting the right finishes

● ● ●

A ROOM'S WINDOWS AND WALLS, FLOORS AND DOORS MAKE UP THE stage for your style. These finishing touches surround your furnishings, showcasing what's in the room and setting the overall scene and mood of the space. Like most of the items you select for this utilitarian space, background materials should look good and work hard to ward off moisture damage, prevent slipping, and keep the room sanitary.

Manufacturers of laminates, tile, stone, paint, fabrics, and wall coverings continue to refine their products from both a design and an engineering point of view. If you haven't shopped the tile aisle recently, you'll be surprised at the candy-store array of colors, shapes, and ingredients. Moisture-resistant fabrics and wall coverings offer a soft and colorful counterpoint to what can be a room of cold and sterile fixtures, just as stone, ceramic, wood, and engineered materials serve up texture and richness to balance the slick side of the space.

Mosaic tiles cast in glass, ceramic, or stone are finding their way onto bathroom walls thanks to the relative ease of installing the tiny tiles, which are sold and installed in multiples on mesh sheets. The watery shades of these prearranged glass tiles add art and sparkle to a guest bath.

budgeting for backgrounds

●●● IT PAYS TO KEEP YOUR BANK BALANCE IN mind when you shop for background elements to finish off your bath, and you'll discover a vast cost spectrum for materials. Plastic, laminates, acrylic, and vinyl products come in a variety of price ranges based on the quality of their materials and designs, but are generally the most cost-efficient. Ceramic and recycled glass tile, engineered stone, and cement are priced for the middle market. Natural stone, such as marble or limestone, stacks up at the high end of choices.

Some homeowners rely on a splurge-and-save strategy when filling in the blank spaces, using dazzling tile on a vanity or focal-point wall, for example, then filling in with pretty paint or other inexpensive elements. Don't forget fabrics and wallpapers; they are also budget-conscious ways to layer more style on a bath. Many designs are created especially for moisture-prone areas and can be affordable ways to work in color and interest.

When deciding on materials, don't forget to factor in the cost of installation, as it varies widely. It's also important to keep in mind how long you'll be living with these backgrounds. While paint is a fickle homeowner's best friend, it's not so practical to rip up and start again with tile or other materials. That doesn't mean you need to settle on the blandest options, but you should consider how adaptable your choices are to style shifts.

With all of today's options, you aren't limited to a standard tile size. Used on the wall and tub surround, these oversized ceramic tiles have a slightly metallic sheen for a textural finish that contrasts the slick surfaces in the room.

TOP LEFT Glass tile was once seen mostly as an accent tile, but now there is a wider variety of shapes, sizes, materials, and price tags. Though it cuts and installs similarly to ceramic tile, because it is translucent, the subsurface must be thin-set and white so as not to impact the final look.

ABOVE Though wallpaper seems like a risky choice in moisture-prone bathrooms, it's actually a fine one if the paper is installed with tight seams and the room is well vented. This black damask paper finishes a dramatic statement in this bath with ebony floors and moldings.

LEFT Scored concrete floors can be polished to a leather-like softness in their natural, taupe finish or stained to mimic other stone tiles. Joined with walls of oversized recycled-glass tile, the look is earthy elegance and the statement is eco-conscious.

ceramic tile

●●● CERAMIC TILE IS THE NUMBER ONE CHOICE for bathroom floors. Today, tile is often seen climbing the walls, creating a focal-point wall or a waterproof wainscot. You pick the color, texture, shape, and size . . . you won't run out of design options with tile. Accent patterns and mosaics are available on precut mesh, making the project even easier for the do-it-yourselfer. Tile lends an upscale, polished look to bathrooms without being too hard on the checkbook . . . unless you splurge on designer tiles.

Once tile is in place, it demands very little maintenance, especially if the grout is properly sealed against staining. When you're planning a tile statement, don't forget to visualize the grid of grout lines inherent in a tile pattern. If you plan to install tile over a large area, all these lines can become dizzying to the eye. Switch to larger tile (which typically gives a room a more contemporary vibe) or match grout carefully with the color of the tile to avoid too much pattern.

When mosaic tile patterns are pre-bonded to mesh—often sold in 1-sq.-ft. sheets—installation is faster and easier. This tile focal-point wall features a variety of sizes, glazes, and colors for a luminous, custom effect.

Porcelain and ceramic tile come in a variety of sizes and finishes. These large Italian porcelain tiles make a contemporary statement, while small tiles offer a more traditional look underfoot.

Unglazed porcelain and ceramic tile have a hand-honed quality that is hard to beat. Select tile in similar colors but in different sizes and finishes for a custom look at an affordable price.

White ceramic tile is a classic choice in the bath, from traditional subway tile to more contemporary squares in a matte finish. Used on the floor and the wainscot, white ceramic offers a quiet background that lets rugs and other accessories pop.

• tile finishes

Where you want to install the tile can help you decide what type to buy. Glazed tile–in both matte and gloss finishes—is a good choice for the bath because it's impervious to water and staining. Highly polished tile is the most durable but is slippery when wet. Be sure to shop for types that are recommended for a floor application, typically a soft-glazed type because the tiles won't get as slippery. Ask to see the manufacturer's specs for a slip-resistance rating to make sure. If you're feeling indulgent, install radiant heating under the tile floor so you land on a warm floor on chilly days.

Those geometry skills from high school will come in handy when you design a floor with ceramic tile. Set in a more complex herringbone pattern, this creamy honed tile adds design energy without upstaging the slipper bath or view out the windows.

Ceramic tile can mimic more expensive stone tile, from copper-veined slate to pure white marble. Large floor tiles with a honed finish are an appropriate choice in this casual, natural bath.

Deco-inspired tile accents and inspires the dressing area in this bath.

More about...
TYPES OF TILE

Chip away at the seemingly endless tile options by first considering the tile's PEI (Porcelain Enamel Institute) rating listed on the manufacturer's specification information. It's not a measurement of quality but rather a code indicating the areas of use recommended by the maker. A PEI 1 rating signals "wall tile only," while a PEI 5 rating is applied to tile designed for "residential or commercial use with heavy foot traffic."

Here are the primary types of tile.

Ceramic tile is usually made from red or white clay and is finished with a glaze that gives it color and pattern. Tiles typically carry a PEI 3 designation, suitable for light to moderate foot traffic. Unglazed tile is porous, so it will need to be sealed before use in a bathroom setting.

Porcelain tile is made by pressing porcelain clays into dense tiles using the dust-press method. It has finer, denser properties than ceramic, making it suitable for heavy traffic areas. Full-body porcelains carry the color and pattern through the entire thickness of the tile.

Quarry tile most often refers to tile extruded from natural clays and shale. These affordable tiles are made for heavy traffic both inside and outside the home, but they need to be glazed or sealed against moisture absorption and staining.

Natural stone tile is usually made from the three stones most suitable for flooring and easiest to cut: marble, granite, and slate. They can be polished (shiny and slippery) or honed (matte and less slippery).

Glass tile has charged into the marketplace in recent years. It can be installed just about anywhere ceramic tile can, though manufacturers recommend using small tile on the floor for more even weight distribution. That way, weight is distributed among many tiles, so there is less chance of breakage. Also, large tile needs to be installed on a perfectly flat floor, while mosaic tiles conform to the floor more easily. Glass tile shouldn't be used on the floor unless it is manufactured for that purpose. Tile with a sandblasted finish keeps glass from being too slippery.

ABOVE Mosaic tiles are sold in prematted sheets so that you have a readymade palette and design. These glass-strip mosaics form a 12-in. border to stud a wall of white subway tile with colorful character.

TOP RIGHT Use tile to highlight special architectural features in your bath. Framed within shallow shower niches, ebony mosaic tile adds visual dimension to this white-tile shower.

RIGHT When you want to create a peaceful bath setting but not a boring one, vary the size of same-colored tile for design interest without the busyness of a lot of pattern or color. Here, 3-in. by 6-in. glass tile in a watery blue shade alternates with 1-in. by 6-in. accent tile.

ABOVE Select ceramic tile with delicate embossed or painted-on designs to create an intriguing border and backsplash for counters or bath decks. Swirling white lines bring art deco modernity to soft gray tile—the perfect complement for a marble counter.

LEFT When tile is a masterpiece of style, keep the rest of the setting hushed to really let its beauty shine. Moroccan ceramic tile is as durable as it is beautiful. It underscores the austere beauty of this guest bath.

glass in the bath

●●● THERE ARE GOOD REASONS WHY GLASS tile has exploded into the bathroom surfaces market: The tiles can be tempered for strength; they can't be breached by moisture or stains; they can be cut, poured, and polished into a variety of shapes and finishes; and they bring a colorful shimmer to your space by reflecting light. Since glass tile is often made from recycled bottles, jars, and other discards, glass even appeals to those with a green bent.

Covering walls, counters, and floors with glass easily relates these surfaces to the other glass elements in the room, from shower doors to mirrored expanses. Pale, watery glass tile unites all these elements for a space with spa-like sparkle. For drama, choose rich and deeply tinted glass tile to temper clear glass.

Glass tile brings a reflective, watery beauty to a bathroom space. Though available at a wider price range than in the past, quality glass tile can be pricey. Use it only on areas you want to highlight to get visual bang for less buck.

The sky is the limit when it comes to decorating walls with tile. In this guest bath—which also serves as the powder room—neutral shades of glass tile create a dramatic mosaic that adds beauty and interest by day or night.

TOP An easy material to cut and color, glass accent tiles come in all shapes and shades. These prematted bubble tiles add an artful and watery contrast to the surrounding large ceramic wall tiles that have a leathery finish.

ABOVE Shimmering glass mosaic tile draws the eye where you want it to go. This pavilion-style shower uses glass mosaic tiles to highlight its dropped ceiling.

•glass tile considerations

There is a trade-off for all of the benefits and beauty of glass. Mineral deposits from water and soap residue cling to glass, making daily upkeep necessary for optimal shine. Fortunately, there are plenty of products and tools to help with this task. Avoid abrasive cleaners on all glass surfaces because they could scratch or dull the surface. For a natural cleaner, try vinegar. Or, for stubborn stains, use orange citrus cleaners.

Like other tile products, shop for glass types that are designed for the location they will be installed. The Tile Council of North America (TCNA) has recently published standards for glass-tile manufacturers, which will be listed in the specs that accompany the product. To find out more on the standards associated with buying or installing tile, visit www.tcnatile.com.

Glass tile can be used effectively as a floor covering. To avoid breakage and to minimize the slippery finish, select mosaic-size tile so the weight is distributed among several tiles.

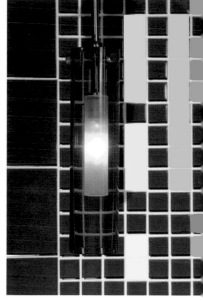

ABOVE Fused glass tile has depth and dimension for dramatic effect, especially when lit by accent lighting. It is made by adding color to the backside of clear glass (usually the sturdy type of glass used in windshields).

LEFT Because it can be precision-cut, glass can be cut into micro mosaic tiles requiring minimal grout lines. On this vanity niche, pale blue mosaics top off the design scheme with a layer of sparkle.

natural stone and stone tile

● ● ● CLASSIC NATURAL MATERIALS SUCH AS granite, marble, limestone, and slate are at the high end of your surfacing options. These earthy offerings make a powerful design statement and are among the strongest surface materials. Your toughest decision may be whether you opt for a honed or polished finish. Honed finishes are matte and less slippery, but the honing process will leave the stone's pores open and prone to dirt build-up and staining unless it's properly sealed. Polishing makes for easier maintenance, but the surface becomes slippery when wet. All stone needs to be resealed on occasion and requires special cleaners to keep it looking its best.

Travertine is a kind of limestone deposited by mineral springs that is dense enough to be considered marble. That strength, plus its more economical price and calming, creamy appearance, makes it a top choice in bathrooms.

TOP Pebble mosaic tile is a natural option that has recently tumbled into the bathroom design market. The natural stone tiles are usually sold in 12-in. × 12-in. mesh sheets, making installation a lot easier than it looks.

ABOVE Iconic marble comes in so many shapes and sizes it can cover virtually every flat surface in the bathroom. On these walls, marble tiles are rectified, or specially cut to butt together tightly, minimizing grout lines. All marble should be sealed before grouting to prevent staining the tiles during grout installation.

Granite weighs in as the stone with the most density and strength, especially high-quality granite. This granite floor tile signals maximum strength and quality with its uniform polishing and even distribution of quartz, feldspar, and mica flecks.

• stone choices

Marble is the hands-down favorite stone for use in the bathroom, and it's been on that pedestal for centuries. Sold in slabs or cut into 1-in. × 1-in. mosaics, marble offers up a huge range of looks, depending on where the stone was mined. No matter its origin, though, marble always exhibits calm, elegant graining and color, running the gamut from almost pure white to dramatic blacks and browns.

Recently, limestone and concrete have been finding their way into the hands of creative homeowners. Limestone is loved for its soft-as-suede appearance. This readily available, sandy stone often captures fossils and other natural beauty marks, making it a good match for casual homes. Like marble, limestone comes in a spectrum of colors and characteristics, depending on where it was mined. Typically, creamy limestone is softer than marble, requiring special sealing and upkeep to counter its absorbent properties.

A more affordable and flexible option for floors, walls, or counters is poured concrete. It can be dyed, molded, and inlaid with fun accents. Use concrete to mimic other, more expensive stones or to make an artful, personal statement. On the down side, concrete can crack if it is not installed properly on flat and unmoving surfaces.

Slate, a natural stone, has a chic black appearance, but has enough texture to make it feel at home in a clean, modern setting or a casual environment. Like all natural stone, slate should be properly sealed and maintained to preserve its good looks—and your investment.

Marble tile gains dimension and luminosity when installed in the classic basketweave pattern. Here, the pattern is played out in soft shades of gray.

Limestone is available in tile and precut slabs. Both types are used effectively in this tranquil master bathroom in the rectified floor tile and the tub backsplash.

ABOVE When cut into tile, marble floors are easier to install—and can be fun to update. Micro accent tiles stud this floor along the grout line for a modern look.

LEFT To make a small room look larger than life, continue the floor pattern into the shower. Marble basketweave tile honed to a mellow finish is more slip-proof than flat marble applications.

vinyl variations

●●● NO MATTER WHAT YOUR DECORATING scheme is, vinyl has you covered. The most popular floor covering found in bathrooms across the United States, versatile vinyl is affordable and available in as many colors and patterns as you can think up. With the new, style-forward (or, in some cases, retro) designs, you don't have to sacrifice style to get the warmth and comfort of vinyl.

Vinyl has always been well suited to bathroom applications because it's moisture-proof and soft underfoot. It's available in both tile and sheet formats, each with its own advantages. Though tile is easier for the do-it-yourselfer to install than sheet vinyl, the seams in tile applications have to be well sealed or they will lift over time. Slip-proof vinyl is a smart choice for bathrooms that will be used by children or the elderly. The flooring comes in a wide range of prices, but keep in mind that the most economical grades will be the first to fade, crack, or show signs of wear.

The latest offerings in vinyl flooring have made great strides in design and engineering, looking more like the real material than ever. This fruitwood look-alike is sold in 48-in. × 4½-in. "planks."

If you think vinyl sheet flooring isn't sophisticated, you should take another look. With uniform shading and a matte finish, this vinyl floor is a dead ringer for chic concrete.

A clean sweep of vinyl sheeting creates an easy-to-maintain flooring surface at a cost far less than tile and stone. Designed as a doppelganger for marble, this gleaming floor is also softer underfoot.

laminates and wood

●●● WARM, NATURAL, AND SOFT UNDERFOOT, wood looks good anywhere. Water can be an enemy to wood, especially when it is allowed to seep into gaps between planks and around walls or fixtures, so when it's used in a bathroom, wood must be sealed against moisture.

Laminate flooring comes together in four layers: a wear layer, a design layer, an inner core, and a backing. The wear layer protects the floor from stains, fading, and moisture. Beneath that, the design layer is literally a digital, photographic image of wood, stone, or another natural material. (Laminates also come in a range of bright hues.) For structural strength, the inner core's plastic layer keeps the laminate stable and flat. Finally, the backing creates a moisture barrier that protects the laminate from warping. All these layers add up to a fine flooring choice in the bathroom.

Eco-conscious bamboo and cork are becoming more common alternatives to more traditional hardwoods. Both types of coverings are made from tree-like tropical grasses that replenish themselves. Bamboo offers the gleaming grains of wood, but it's a harder material that also resists moisture. Cork offers a soft, pliable feel underfoot and stands up to water well, especially when sealed with water-based polyurethane. Both cork and bamboo are naturally resistant to mildew and bacteria.

Hardwood or laminate floors create continuity between bedrooms and bathrooms. That's especially important in open floor plans, such as this lofty suite.

FAR LEFT When properly sealed and installed, hardwood floors are a fine way to underscore a bathroom with a casual, organic feel. Even soft pine such as this will stand up to moisture, and it's a natural companion to stone and ceramic tile.

LEFT For a space rooted in natural colors and finishes, the gleaming grains of an oak floor fit right in. Paired with chocolate-colored paint and a built-in vanity, the floor plays a supporting role here whereas another surface choice might have upstaged the quiet design.

Ebonized wood floors make a glamorous statement while underscoring and visually connecting a room's other elements. With surface materials that include a glass-tile shower wall and shades of gray and black paint, this room has a subtle elegance.

wall coverings

●●● NOW ENGINEERED TO BE MILDEW PROOF and cleanable, wall coverings are a practical choice for bathrooms. Even better, they're design problem solvers. With the right pattern, you can alter the perception of a space. Wallpaper with a large motif, for example, will make a room feel more intimate and dramatic. To make a small space appear larger, choose a subtle, airy pattern. If you want to visually raise the roof on a bathroom with low ceilings, check out vertical stripes.

Stripes, checks, and other geometric patterns can lend a nondescript room a sense of architecture. Need a little texture to counter all the slick surfaces in the bath? Shop for grass-cloth coverings or other wallpapers that lend textural interest. Before you settle on a pattern, consider how much tolerance for visual busyness you have. If you don't know for sure, take a cue from your closet—if you have a lot of clothes with patterns, you probably would like a bold pattern on your walls.

A pretty paper might be all you need to put a dated or dull bath in a new light. With its fun frog motif and happy colors, this wall covering is chosen for its Lily Pulitzer–style freshness.

Vintage-style wallpapers can reinforce a traditional scheme. In a stylized paisley pattern, this paper underscores the light Victorian feel established by the decorative sink and commode.

Contrary to one decorating myth, bold wallpaper patterns can look fabulous in small rooms. Limit the pattern to the upper wall or a single wall so you don't overpower the space.

Keep a peaceful, easy feeling in a room by selecting paper with a pale background and an airy pattern. The star motifs of this design have a glint of silver to play off the glass-tile shower wall.

RIGHT Any type of paper will stick to the wall under the right conditions. These homeowners affixed their home's floor plans to a powder room that doesn't see a lot of humidity.

BELOW Installed from floor to ceiling, wallpaper makes an exposed, under-sink area look more finished. Look for wall coverings that boast a scrubbable finish to be certain you can chase after soap and watermarks, or the errant lipstick slash.

Frame an artful wall covering with simple moldings to add elegance to your backgrounds. This design technique adds character in a small bathroom without windows.

painted surfaces

●●● PAINT GETS THE PRIZE FOR THE PRODUCT that creates the most drama with the least amount of cash. No wonder a bucket of paint is considered the home decorator's best friend. Turns out, paint is also an excellent surface covering, even in the busiest, wettest bathroom…if you choose the right paint.

Sheen is the most important consideration when you shop for paint. Semi-gloss and high-gloss paints are less porous than flat or eggshell finishes, making them more resistant to humidity and cracking. When paint lifts on drywall, serious mildew problems can creep underneath. Glossy paints are also easier to clean. Priming the walls with a product that contains mildew-resistant additives helps prevent unhealthy mold growth.

While high-gloss paints are generally a good choice for bathrooms, they do have one disadvantage—they show a wall's imperfections more than flat finishes. If your walls are worse for wear, use flat paints with mildew-resistant additives mixed in. You can also mix your own by buying the additive separately and adding it to your favorite paint.

Frame white cabinetry and fixtures in a soft brush of color. If you want a flat, matte look, get paint in a washable finish.

TOP LEFT Paint can transform simple paneling constructed of affordable woods into a richer, more elegant style statement. The gleaming gold-painted moldings in this room cap off an eclectic mixture of glass and aged woods.

ABOVE Dramatic strokes of color give small bathrooms a more powerful presence. Select earth shades, such as this terra cotta, to create surroundings that complement skin tones.

LEFT Paint paneling white for a comfortable, cottage style. For a more modern take on this classic look, these walls are treated to flat, plank paneling installed horizontally.

•color considerations

Color can change a room's mood . . . and yours! Many correlations between color and mood are obvious: Orange and red are more energetic colors, while pale blues and soft greens evoke calm. Think about the kind of feeling you want the space to give off to you or your guests to help you narrow your color choices.

Another thing to think about is how color looks around you. For most skin tones, cosmetic pinks, creams, coppers, and peaches are the most flattering shades.

ABOVE A small bathroom is a good place to be more daring with color. Hedge your bets by pulling from nature's palette. In this pint-size powder room, grassy green is balanced by sidewalls in bark brown.

LEFT Paint walls in varying shades to add dimension to a space and to highlight key design elements. By painting the middle plane butternut and the rest of the walls gray, these homeowners highlighted the shower's architecture.

FACING PAGE If you need help narrowing down a palette, pull pretty shades from your bedroom wallpaper into the bathroom. For a chic update on mid-century modern, glass tile takes over for ceramic in retro aqua shades.

fabrics

●●● NOTHING SOFTENS THE SHARP EDGES AND sleek surfaces of a bathroom like folds of flowing fabric. Whether it's draped across a window or stretched across a shower, fabric is a pretty way to link a bathroom with an adjacent bedroom or to simply add more personality to the space.

If you've been looking, you've likely noticed that shower curtains have taken a big design leap forward. From graphic motifs to detailed line drawings to fluid folds of bright solids, shower curtains are sporting artful and unique motifs. These fabrics are machine washable and, with regular care, resist mold. Most machine-washable fabrics hold up well in the humid environment, as long as they don't get soaking wet regularly. For hard-wearing, water-resistant options for fabrics that see heavy use, check out the vast array of indoor/outdoor fabrics, all of which have a softer hand and crisper, more colorful designs than in years past.

ABOVE AND RIGHT Decorative readymade or custom shower curtains can mask a standard bath or add soft color and pattern. This custom curtain features eye-catching streams of ribbon, embroidered stitching, and a vinyl lining.

ABOVE For instant color and structure in a bath, turn to classic stripe patterns. Stripes are a great choice in bathroom schemes that need to "grow up" with a child.

LEFT Area rugs and accent fabrics belong in bathrooms, not just living rooms. Most natural fibers hold up fine in bathrooms that have the proper ventilation, as long as they don't get soaked.

· window coverings

The need for privacy in the bath is a no-brainer, but your window dressing can do much more than simply protect your privacy. Window treatments can softly frame a sculptural freestanding tub, direct natural light, or add energy efficiency. You can also make a wimpy window more dramatic or protect an in-shower window from moisture. Think about how you want a curtain, blind, or shade to function before you settle on a choice.

ABOVE Many readymade shades and blinds are moisture-resistant polyester and vinyl materials, making them a good choice for bathrooms—even when your windows are near a bathroom's water source. These Roman shades have a soft but tidy appearance, controlling light and privacy without masking the window's architecture.

RIGHT Pretty cotton fabrics make a clean, crisp statement in a bathroom, while offering privacy and filtering light to a diffused glow. With seersucker detailing, this natural cotton fabric brings a summery feeling to this bath.

FAR RIGHT Pleated shades filter light to a soft glow and add insulation. They're a good choice in bathrooms, where privacy is needed but heavy window treatments are not.

Plantation shutters made from finished or painted wood or from wood-composite materials can withstand the humidity in a properly vented bathroom. Their classic, cottage charm adds to the architectural character of any space.

light, heat, and ventilation

• • •

LIGHTING, HEATING, AND VENTILATION MAY NOT BE THE MOST EXCITING elements in the bathroom, but they are central to how comfortable your remodeled space will be. The right mix of task and ambient lighting will help ensure you are looking your best in the morning and can relax in a room softened to a warm glow at night. Heated towel bars and floor tiles add a layer of spa-like luxury that will literally warm you to your toes. And the right venting system will whisk away moisture to make it easier on you and your room. A thoughtful combination of heating and ventilation will make sure you don't step out of a hot tub or shower only to stand and shiver, or feel as if you're dripping in a steam room instead of your own home.

Don't forget to factor in natural light. Windows, transoms, and skylights assist in both lighting and venting the room—and they are defining design elements in the room's finished look. Discuss windows with your contractor based on your need to frame a view and to secure daytime (and nighttime!) privacy, as well as air movement and light.

Spend some time thinking of these three key components. In the end, they will make your new bath feel as good as it looks.

Multiple sources of light and heat, both natural and artificial, mean multiple sources of comfort. This Texas bathroom takes advantage of solar benefits through a high bank of windows.

illuminating ideas

●●● WHEN PUTTING TOGETHER A LIGHTING plan, try to include options for natural and artificial light. Daylighting—capturing natural light through windows or skylights—can save you money on your energy bill when it offers up the main source of light during daytime hours. Even better, windows invite in the beauty and warmth of sunshine.

Artificial lighting is categorized into three basic types: task, accent, or ambient lighting. A good interior lighting plan will layer in all three types. Task lighting is functional, concentrated light that assists you in performing a close task. In the bathroom, vanity lighting falls into this category. Accent lighting is mainly decorative, intended to highlight special design elements in a room. Ambient, or general, lighting fills in from there, offering up illumination for an entire room. Ceiling fixtures are examples of ambient light.

Lighting acts like the jewelry of a room, adding a final layer of sparkle and decoration. Vanity lights, a chandelier, and recessed lights are pretty and practical accents in this Chicago master bathroom.

This master bathroom has multiple sources of natural and artificial light. An operational window in the shower ushers in daylight for a warm start to the morning. The window also draws out humidity, where it won't damage surfaces that aren't moisture resistant, such as drywall.

TOP A lighted cosmetic mirror is a perfect example of task lighting in the bathroom. This wall-mounted type swings where it's needed to offer backup to the vertical sidelights. Vertical tubes of light do the best job of lighting the face evenly.

ABOVE A bank of high transom windows lets daylight fill a bathroom, without worries about privacy. Creamy yellow hues further the sunny feeling here.

•task lighting

Task lighting in the bathroom puts the spotlight on close-up duties such as shaving, applying cosmetics, and grooming. This type of lighting typically translates to vanity fixtures. Ideally, sidelights should flank the mirror at eye level about 36 in. apart to prevent distracting shadows on the face. Lights placed above the mirror don't illuminate the face as evenly. If your room doesn't allow for sidelights or sconces, consider installing a light above the mirror that is at least 24 in. long to spread the light more evenly across the face. The most common lighting mistake in the bathroom is putting ceiling fixtures directly over the mirror, which will cast harsh shadows on the face.

Depending on the size of the room and the floor plan, task lighting might also be needed in the shower and tub or toilet area for both safety and illumination. Shop for recessed lights with special shower trims to ensure the fixtures can handle the high humidity.

Experts recommend light bulbs that contain 150 watts of power to handle tasks in the bath. Put lights on a dimmer to leave you in control of your lighting effects. This way, task lighting can soften into mood lighting when you want it to. Plus, dimmers will also save energy and money and extend the life of traditional bulbs.

Light casings made to withstand high humidity are a must in showers. If a shower isn't well lit by other sources in the room, recessed lighting is needed for function and safety.

TOP LEFT Task lighting needn't look as utilitarian as it sounds. This sconce features a graceful, arching post that puts it in the perfect spot for lighting the mirror and the glass-encased shower.

ABOVE Strategic placement of glass and mirrors will make the most of the light a room receives. This water closet is fabricated with translucent glass so light can funnel in from windows and other sources in the room.

LEFT If wall space doesn't allow you to install vanity lights to each side of the mirror, putting a task light up high is the way to go. Horizontal tubes of light will spread light evenly across the face if they stretch close to the width of the mirror.

•ambient and accent light

Ambient light is a kind of fill-in light that is considered a substitute for natural light. This type of light is usually supplied by ceiling-mounted fixtures. For extra sparkle and style, consider opting out of a standard ceiling fixture and shopping for an eye-catching chandelier or a colorful pendant.

Small lights aimed at special artwork or at an architectural element create another layer of light in the bath. Spotlights can also be directed to wash across a distinctive wall of tile or a special basin.

RIGHT Cleverly placed recessed lights and spotlights serve up ambient and accent lighting at the same time. Note how a small spotlight highlights a favorite piece of art, while a larger recessed light sends beams to glass shelves and then bounces around the room. Glass and mirrors maximize your light.

FACING PAGE TOP A decorative pendant light or chandelier does much more than provide ambient light; it lends unexpected style and a personal touch. Put lights on dimmers so you can control the mood of the room.

LEFT One inexpensive lighting trick to gain ambient light is to tuck rope lights atop cabinets, beams, or moldings. Here, the lights call attention to a vaulted ceiling.

More about...
WHAT BULB TO CHOOSE

make sure you're putting your best face forward by getting the light right. You want a crisp, white light, which presents skin tones most accurately.

Halogen bulbs produce the clearest light. Low-voltage types (with a built-in transformer that converts 120 volts to 12 volts) are compact and efficient to operate. Halogen bulbs cost 10 to 20 percent more than incandescent varieties but typically last three times as long. Many bulbs feature screw-in bases, but those labeled "medium-base" (MB) fit any standard light fixture.

The newest compact fluorescent bulbs (CFL) offer cleaner light than in years past, eliminating the unflattering green cast. They're also up to 10 times more efficient than the once-standard incandescent.

Light bulb manufacturers are now required to meet government efficiency standards to reduce consumers' energy usage and air pollution created by the burning of fossil fuels. Under the Energy Independence and Security Act of 2007, a 72-watt incandescent halogen bulb or a 23-watt compact fluorescent bulb must replace, and be as bright as, a traditional 100-watt incandescent bulb.

ABOVE When a room seems lacking in architectural interest, conjure up a focal point with the help of accent lighting. A simple niche inset between wall studs offers a spot of grace without marring the Zen simplicity of the room, thanks to metallic paint and an accent light.

RIGHT Skylights prevent a windowless bathroom from becoming a dark tunnel day or night. Accent lights installed under wall-mounted vanities add a warm glow and a greater sense of openness.

TOP Hang pendant lights in front of a mirror for double the light. Amber shades cast a warm, flattering glow on skin tones.

ABOVE In bathrooms without windows or other natural light sources, add warmth with lighting and texture. In this basement bathroom, textural wall coverings get notice with a wash of light from recessed halogens installed in a header box.

Like other design elements in the home, select lighting fixtures that share finishes or styles with those in adjoining rooms for visually pleasing design continuity. This pendant fixture relates to the bedroom ceiling light without matching perfectly.

climate
control

●●● OF ALL THE ROOMS OF THE HOUSE, THE bathroom is the one in which you want to maintain the most control of temperature and humidity. That's because it's the one in which you spend a good deal of time undressed. Exposed skin is sensitive to water and air (and floor!) temperature, to the moisture in the air, and even to the heat of the toilet seat.

Such basic sensations direct many of the decisions as you plan any bath renovation or building project. Fans, a supplemental floor heating system, and water fixtures with thermostatic valves are all items that should be on your punch list to ensure a comfortable atmosphere. Many of these items, thankfully, are not expensive.

A two-way fireplace installed into a wall between a master bedroom and bath brings resort-level luxury to everyday life. This custom unit is pricey, but there are plug-in options at all prices.

LEFT In nature, stone and ceramic surfaces absorb heat from the sun by day and release it back into the environment long after the sun goes down. Sunny windows mean this trick works inside, too.

BELOW Counter the cold surfaces in a bathroom with touches of warmth. Towel warmers heat both the air and the towels for luxurious warmth in this marble-clad bath. The recessed lights use heat bulbs to further warm the bathing area.

• temperature

Simple experience tells us that it's more comfortable to keep the bathroom slightly warmer than the rest of house, especially when you'll be stepping out of the shower or bath. There are a number of ways to make this happen, but a continuing trend in bath design is the installation of radiant floor heating. To get that pampered feeling of stepping onto a floor that seems heated by sunrays, you will generally spend less than $1,000 to install an electric radiant system in the limited space of a bathroom.

If radiant floor heat isn't feasible, consider the little luxuries available to heat up your room, such as a recessed heat light, plug-in heater, or towel-warming drawer. Wall-mounted towel racks also keep a toasty towel at the ready. There are plug-in types or more elaborate systems that can be wired into your room's electrical system. If the sky's the limit—and you have enough square footage—design the space to include a gas fireplace.

Keep warm towels within reach when you want them with towel-warming bars set up on a timer. Creamy colors and natural light do their part to add warmth in this traditional bath, but a heated towel waiting right outside the shower door is the ultimate little luxury.

More about...
WATER AND ELECTRICITY

i t's common knowledge that water and electricity don't mix. To keep them separate in the bath's mechanical systems, consider these highlights from the National Electrical code published by the U.S. National Fire Protection Association.

- Install only GFCI (ground fault circuit interrupter) receptacles in bathrooms.

- There must be a receptacle within 3 ft. of the outside edge of the sink basin.

- No plug receptacle should be installed face up on a horizontal bath surface.

- Receptacles must be on at least one separate 20-amp branch circuit in the home's electrical panel because of the use of high-wattage appliances such as hair dryers.

ABOVE Gas fireplaces feature blowers to help spread the warmth around the room. This small, direct-vent unit heats both the bedroom and bathroom.

RIGHT Ceramic, porcelain, concrete, and stone are all candidates for radiant floor heating systems. Grout lines must be sealed against moisture to prevent electric shocks when water hits them.

• humidity

Without a properly powered exhaust fan to clear the air, humid air from hot baths and steamy showers will inevitably lead to mold or mildew—and eventually rot if the room is chronically damp. Ideally, you should install a fan that has a feature that engages the motor automatically at a preset humidity level. Using fans with timer switches is another good way to ensure that the bath is free of moisture. Timers also prevent the needless waste of energy when the fan is inadvertently left on.

Fans are rated according to the volume of air they can move per minute (known as CFM, or cubic feet per minute). As a guideline, a small bath should have a fan rated at 50 CFM; a larger bath over 100 sq. ft. will need 100 CFM or more. Pay attention to noise, too. Fan sound is measured in sones; look for one rated 1 sone or less.

ABOVE AND LEFT Fans designed for installation directly in the shower will whisk away moist air to the great outdoors. The size of fan you need is determined by your room's square footage. This small fan is flanked by two waterproof recessed lights.

LEFT Open showers allow steam to escape and dissipate into the larger area of the room. This glass shower stall—along with the large mirror—also allows light to bounce around to add sparkle throughout the space.

BELOW In this classic bath, a window between the shower and tub can be left open for venting or closed tight to convert a standard shower into a steam bath.

resources

ASSOCIATIONS

The American Institute of Architects
1735 New York Ave. NW
Washington, DC 20006-5292
800-AIA-3837
www.aia.org

American Society of Interior Designers (ASID)
608 Massachusetts Ave. NE
Washington, DC 20002-60006
202-546-3480
www.asid.org

Consumer Reports
101 Truman Ave.
Yonkers, NY 10703-1057
866-208-9427
www.consumerreports.org

National Association of Home Builders
1201 15th St. NW
Washington, DC 20005
800-368-5242
www.nahb.org

National Association of the Remodeling Industry (NARI)
P.O. Box 4250
Des Plaines, IL 60016
847-298-9225
www.nari.org

National Kitchen & Bath Association
687 Willow Grove St.
Hackettstown, NJ 07840
800-843-6522
www.nkba.org

National Wood Flooring Association
111 Chesterfield Industrial Blvd.
Chesterfield, MO 63005
636-519-9663
www.woodfloors.org

Plumbing-Heating-Cooling Contractors Association
180 S. Washington St.
Falls Church, VA 22046
800-533-7694
www.phccweb.org

The Tile Council of North America
100 Clemson Research Blvd.
Anderson, SC 29625
864-646-8453
www.tcnatile.com

U.S. Green Building Council
2101 L St. NW
Suite 500
Washington, DC 20037
800-795-1747
www.usgbc.org
www.greenhomeguide.com

INDUSTRY LEADERS

American Standard
Customer Care
1 Centennial Plaza
Piscataway, NJ 08855-6820
800-442-1902
www.americanstandard-us.com

Ann Sacks Tile
800-278-8453
www.annsacks.com

Armstrong World Industries
2500 Columbia Ave.
P.O. Box 3001
Lancaster, PA 17604
717-397-0611
www.armstrong.com

Crossville, Inc.
P.O. Box 1168
Crossville, TN 38557
931-484-2110
www.crossvilleinc.com

Eljer
Customer Service
41 Cairns Rd.
Mansfield, OH 44904
800-442-1902
www.eljer.com

Grohe America, Inc.
241 Covington Dr.
Bloomingdale, IL 60108
630-582-7711
www.groheamerica.com

The Home Depot
Customer Care
800-466-3337
www.homedepot.com

Kohler Co.
444 Highland Dr.
Kohler, WI 53044
800-456-4537
www.kohler.com

Lowes
Customer Care
P.O. Box 1111
North Wilkesboro, NC 28656-001
800-445-6937
www.lowes.com

Wilsonart International, Inc.
2400 Wilson Place
P.O. Box 6110
Temple, TX 76503-6110
800-433-3222
www.wilsonart.com

photo credits

pp. ii-iii: © Eric Roth

p. v: © Eric Roth

p. vi: © Eric Roth, design: www. paynebouchier.com (top left and bottom left); © Hulya Kolabas, design: Vicki Taylor-Bloch and Donna Sexton AtHome Design LLC (top right); © Hulya Kolabas, design: Coastal Properties, LLC (bottom right)

p. 1: © Hulya Kolabas, design: Granoff Architecture (top left); © Eric Roth, design: www.trikeenan.com (top right); © Ryann Ford (bottom)

pp. 2-3: © Eric Roth, design: www. svdesign.com (left); © Eric Roth, design: www.brittadesign.com (center); © Mark Lohman, design: Little Crown Interiors (right)

CHAPTER 1

p. 4: © Eric Roth, design: www. paynebouchier.com

p. 6: © Eric Roth, design: www. renovationplanning.com (top); © Eric Roth, design: www.hutkerarchitects.com (bottom)

p. 7: © Hulya Kolabas, design: Granoff Architecture

p. 8: © Mark Lohman, design: Cynthia Marks Interior Design

p. 9: © Ryann Ford (top left); © Eric Roth, design: www.zeroenergy.com (bottom left); © Doug Smith, design: Mark Radosevich, MR Construction, Des Moines, IA, 515-225-3577 (right)

p. 10: © Susan Teare, design/build: Conner & Buck, color: Mitra Designs

p. 11: © Eric Roth (left); © Anne Gummerson, design: Interior Design by Jan Angevine, Baltimore, MD, Architecture by Brennan and Company, Architects, Ellicott City, MD, 410-313-8310, www. brennanarch.com (right)

p. 12: © Hulya Kolabas

p. 13: © Eric Roth (left); © Ryann Ford, design: Paul DeGroot, Architect, www. degrootarchitect.com (right)

p. 14: © Tria Giovan, design: Phillip Sides

p. 15: © Eric Roth (top and bottom)

p. 16: © Anne Gummerson, design: Penza-Bailey Architects, Baltimore

p. 17: © Hulya Kolabas, design: Neil Hauck Architects (left); © Mark Lohman,

design: Barclay Butera Inc. (top right); © Doug Smith, design: Mark Radosevich, MR Construction, Des Moines, IA, 515-225-3577 (bottom right)

p. 18: © Hulya Kolabas, design: CWB Architects

p. 19: © Hulya Kolabas, design: Vicki Taylor-Bloch and Donna Sexton AtHome Design LLC (top); © Eric Roth (bottom)

p. 20: © Eric Roth (top and bottom)

p. 21: © Ryann Ford, design: Paul DeGroot, Architect, www.degrootarchitect. com (top); © Eric Roth (bottom)

p. 22: © Eric Roth, design: www. howellcustombuild.com

p. 23: © Susan Teare, design: Cushman Design Group (top left); © Tria Giovan (top right); © Eric Roth (bottom)

p. 24: © Eric Roth, design: www. pamelacopeman.com (left); © Hulya Kolabas, design: Delson or Sherman Architects PC

p. 25: © Hulya Kolabas, design: Stacey Gendelman Interior Design (top left); © Eric Roth, design: www. geraldpomeroydesigngroup.com (bottom left); © Eric Roth (right)

p. 26: © Eric Roth

p. 27: © Hulya Kolabas, design: Stacey Gendelman Interior Design (top); © Eric Roth

p. 28: © Eric Roth, design: www. svdesign.com (top); © Hulya Kolabas (bottom left); © Eric Roth, design: www. duffydesigngroup.com (bottom right)

p. 29: © Eric Roth (left); © Hulya Kolabas (right)

p. 30: © Hulya Kolabas, design: CWB Architects (left); © Eric Roth, design: www. markfinlay.com (right)

p. 31: © Eric Roth (top and bottom)

p. 32: © Eric Roth, design: ruhlwalker.com (left); © Hulya Kolabas, design: Stacey Gendelman Interior Design

p. 33: © Ryann Ford (top left); © Hulya Kolabas, design: Lorrie Abonavontura Architecture (bottom left); © Eric Roth (right)

CHAPTER 2

p. 34: © Hulya Kolabas, design: Vicki Taylor-Bloch and Donna Sexton AtHome Design LLC

p. 36: © Eric Roth, design: www.trikeenan. com

p. 40: © Anne Gummerson, design: Jay B. Huyett, AIA, Studio 3 Architecture/ Studio Snaidero DC, 410-693-1590, jay@ studio3architectureinc.com

p. 41: © Ryann Ford (top left); © Doug Smith, design: Mark Radosevich, MR Construction, Des Moines, IA, 515-225-3577 (bottom left); © Hulya Kolabas, design: CWB Architects (right)

p. 42: © Eric Roth

p. 43: © Hulya Kolabas, design: CWB Architects

p. 44: © Eric Roth

p. 45: © Eric Roth, design: www. daherinteriordesign.com (left); © Eric Roth (right)

p. 46: © Eric Roth

p. 47: © Eric Roth, design: www. paynebouchier.com (left); © Hulya Kolabas, design: Bartels-Pagliaro Architects (right)

p. 48: © Eric Roth, design: www. adamsbeasley.com (left); © Hulya Kolabas (top right); © Eric Roth, design: www. paynebouchier.com (bottom right)

p. 49: © Hulya Kolabas, design: CWB Architects (left); © Ryann Ford (right)

p. 50: © Matthew Gilson, design: Rebekah Zaveloff, KitchenLab, LLC, Design in a Bag, www.designinabag.com (left); © Susan Teare, design: Dan Memont of Design Dynamics in Mass. (right)

p. 51: © Hulya Kolabas, design: Richard Swan Architect

p. 52: Photoshot/Red Cover/Christopher Drake (top); © Eric Roth (bottom)

p. 53: © Susan Teare, design: Studio III architects, Gregory C. Masefield Jr. AIA, NCARB, Silver Maple Construction, Bristol, VT, Vermont Eco-Floors, Topcoat Finishes

p. 54: © Anne Gummerson, design: Frederick Sieracki, Architect, Annapolis, MD

p. 55: © Anne Gummerson, design: HBF plus Design, Baltimore

p. 56: © Ryann Ford (left and right)

p. 57: © Eric Roth; design: www. gpschafer.com

CHAPTER 3

p. 58: © Eric Roth, design: www. paynebouchier.com

p. 60: © Anne Gummerson, design: HWA, Hammond-Wilson Architects, Annapolis, MD, 410-267-6041, hammondwilsonarchitects.com

p. 61: © Ryann Ford (left); © Susan Teare, design: Studio III architects, Gregory C. Masefield Jr. AIA, NCARB, Silver Maple Construction, Bristol, VT, Vermont Eco Floors, Topcoat Finishes (right)

p. 62: © Ryann Ford (left); © Eric Roth, design: www.lizcaan.com (right)

p. 63: © Eric Roth

p. 64: © Eric Roth, design: Onthank Designs (left); © Ryann Ford

p. 65: © Ryann Ford

p. 66: © Eric Roth

p. 67: © Hulya Kolabas, design: Stacey Gendelman Interior Design (top); © Eric Roth, design: www.hutkerarchitects.com (bottom)

p. 68: © Ryann Ford (top); © Anne Gummerson, design: Inez Schapiro, Interior Designer, Jenkins-Baer Associates, Baltimore, jenkinsbaer.com; architect Shellie Curry, Currie Architects, Baltimore (bottom)

p. 69: © Hulya Kolabas (left); © Ryann Ford (right)

p. 70: © Hulya Kolabas, design: CWB Architects

p. 71: © Mark Lohman (top left); © Ryann Ford (top right); © Eric Roth (bottom)

p. 72: © Eric Roth (top); © Anne Gummerson, design: Coppermine Terrace Interiors, Baltimore (bottom left); © Eric Roth, design: www.christofiinteriors.com (bottom right)

p. 73: © Hulya Kolabas, design: Lauren Muse Interiors + Christina Murphy Interiors

p. 74: © Eric Roth, design: Dressing Rooms (left); © Tria Giovan (right)

p. 75: © Ryann Ford

p. 76: © Mark Lohman (top left); © Eric Roth (top right and bottom)

p. 77: © Ryann Ford

p. 78: © Hulya Kolabas (left); © Eric Roth (right)

p. 79: © Eric Roth, design: www. hutkerarchitects.com (top); © Eric Roth (bottom)

p. 80: © Ryann Ford (left); © Anne Gummerson, design: Julie and Ken Girardini, Sykesville, MD (www. girardinidesign.com) (right)

p. 81: courtesy Paul DeGrout (top); © Eric Roth, design: bkarch.com (bottom)

p. 82: © Ryann Ford (left); © Eric Roth, design: www.paynebouchier.com (top right); © Anne Gummerson, design: Joe Architect and Company, Baltimore, 410-908-6753, www.joe-architect.com, Interior Designer Dan Proctor, Kirk Designs, Inc., Baltimore, www.kirk-designs.com (bottom right)

p. 83: © Hulya Kolabas, design: Jefferey Matz Architects

p. 84: © Mark Lohman, design: Janet Lohman Interior Design

p. 85: © Tria Giovan, design: Betty Wasserman (top and bottom)

p. 86: © Eric Roth (top and bottom)

p. 87: © Mark Lohman, design: Barclay Butera Inc.

p. 88: © Eric Roth

p. 89: © Eric Roth, design: www. jwconstructioninc.com (top left); © Mark Lohman, design: Barclay Butera Inc. (top right); © Eric Roth (bottom)

p. 90: © Hulya Kolabas

p. 91: © Eric Roth, design: www. jwconstructioninc.com (top); © Tria Giovan, design: Phillip Sides (bottom)

CHAPTER 4

p. 92: © Hulya Kolabas, design: Coastal Properties, LLC

p. 94: © Eric Roth, design: www. christinetuttle.com (left); © Ryann Ford, design: Paul DeGroot, Architect, www. degrootarchitect.com (right)

p. 95: © Eric Roth, design: Robert T. Bowman Builder

p. 96: © Eric Roth

p. 97: © Hulya Kolabas, design: Mar Silver Design (top); © Eric Roth, design: www. heidipribell.com (bottom)

p. 98: © Eric Roth, design: www. daherinteriordesign.com (top); © Eric Roth (bottom)

p. 99: © Eric Roth, design: Abby Yozell Unlimited (top); © Ryann Ford (bottom)

p. 100: © Eric Roth (top); © Eric Roth, design: www.jaxtimer.com (bottom)

p. 101: © Hulya Kolabas, design: Richard Swan Architect (top); © Eric Roth, design: www.jwconstructioninc.com (bottom)

p. 102: © Hulya Kolabas, design: Advent Design (top); © Eric Roth, design: www. jwconstructioninc.com (bottom)

p 103: © Hulya Kolabas, design: Jefferey Matz Architects (left); © Ryann Ford (right)

p. 104: © Ryann Ford, design: Paul DeGroot, Architect, www.degrootarchitect. com (top); © Hulya Kolabas, design: Alisberg Parker Architects (bottom)

p. 105: © Hulya Kolabas, design: Vicki Taylor-Bloch and Donna Sexton AtHome Design LLC (left); © Mark Lohman, design: Janet Lohman Interior Design (top right); © Hulya Kolabas, design: Waterworks (bottom right)

p. 106: © Ryann Ford

p. 107: © Eric Roth, design: www. gabourybuilding.com (left); © Eric Roth (top right); © Eric Roth, design: www. renovationplanning.com (bottom right)

p. 108: © Eric Roth, design: www. spacecraftarch.com (left); © Eric Roth, design: www.hutkerarchitects.com (right)

p. 109: © Eric Roth, design: bkarch.com

p. 110: © Eric Roth, design: www. christinetuttle.com

p. 111: © Hulya Kolabas, design: Stacey Gendelman Interior Design (top left); © Hulya Kolabas, design: Granoff Architecture (top right); © Doug Smith, design: Kabira Cadogan, designer, iN/2/iT Design Studio, 515-238-5647 (bottom left)

p. 112: © Hulya Kolabas, design: www. sternmccafferty.com/ (top); © Eric Roth (bottom)

p. 113: © Eric Roth, design: Barbara Boardman

p. 114: © Eric Roth, design: www. paynebouchier.com (top); © Mark Lohman (bottom)

p. 115: © Eric Roth, design: www. gabourybuilding.com

p. 116: © Ryann Ford

p. 117: © Eric Roth (top left); © Ryann Ford (top right); © Tria Giovan (bottom)

p. 118: © Hulya Kolabas, design: Vicki Taylor-Bloch and Donna Sexton AtHome Design LLC (left); © Hulya Kolabas, design: CWB Architects (right)

p. 119: © Eric Roth, design: Robert T. Bowman Builder (top); © Doug Smith, design: Kabira Cadogan, designer, iN/2/iT Design Studio, 515-238-5647 (bottom)

p. 120: © Eric Roth

p. 121: © Eric Roth, design: www.brittadesign.com (top); © Eric Roth, design: www.svdesign.com (bottom)

p. 122: © Eric Roth, design: www.jwconstructioninc.com (left); © Hulya Kolabas, design: Advent Design (right)

p. 123: © Eric Roth, design: www.gabourybuilding.com (top); © Eric Roth, design: baypointbuilderscorp.com (bottom)

p. 124: © Eric Roth (top); © Susan Teare, design: Cushman Design Group (bottom left); © Mark Lohman (bottom right)

p. 125: © Eric Roth, design: Robert T. Bowman Builder

p. 126: © Hulya Kolabas, design: Richard Swan Architect (left); © Eric Roth, design: www.pamelacopeman.com (top right); © Hulya Kolabas (bottom right)

p. p. 127: © Matthew Gilson, design: Rebekah Zaveloff, KitchenLab, LLC, Design in a Bag, www.designinabag.com (top); © Anne Gummerson, design: Julie and Ken Girardini, Sykesville, MD (www.girardinidesign.com) (bottom left); © Mark Lohman, design: Rohl (bottom right)

p. 128: © Hulya Kolabas, design: CWB Architects (left); © Eric Roth, design: www.pamelacopeman.com (right)

p. 129: © Eric Roth, design: Abby Yozell Unlimited (left); © Eric Roth, design: www.jwconstructioninc.com (right)

p. 130: © Hulya Kolabas, design: CWB Architects (top); © Eric Roth (bottom)

p. 131: © Eric Roth (top and bottom)

CHAPTER 5

p. 132: © Hulya Kolabas, design: Granoff Architecture

p. 134: © Eric Roth, design: Erling Falck Architecture & Design

p. 135: © Eric Roth, design: ERS Design (left); © Ryann Ford, design: Paul DeGroot, Architect, www.degrootarchitect.com (top right); © Doug Smith, design: Mark Radosevich, MR Construction, Des Moines, IA, 515-225-3577 (bottom right)

p. 136: © Hulya Kolabas, design: Christopher Peacock Cabinetry (top); ©

Anne Gummerson, design: Alt Breeding Schwarz Architects, Annapolis, MD (bottom)

p. 137: © Doug Smith, design: Kabira Cadogan, designer, iN/2/iT Design Studio, 515-238-5647

p. 138: © Mark Lohman, design: Barclay Butera Inc. (top left); © Eric Roth, design: www.daherinteriordesign.com (top right); © Anne Gummerson, design: HBF plus Design, Baltimore (bottom left); © Ryann Ford (bottom right)

p. 139: © Eric Roth, design: www.brittadesign.com

p. 140: © Anne Gummerson, design: Jay B. Huyett, AIA, Studio 3 Architecture/Studio Snaidero DC, 410-693-1590, jay@studio3architectureinc.com

p. 141: © Hulya Kolabas, design: Stacey Gendelman Interior Design (left); © Eric Roth (top right); Susan Teare, design: Peregrine Design/Build (bottom right)

p. 142: © Eric Roth, design: Sacris Design (top); © Mark Lohman, design: Michael Lee Architects (bottom)

p. 143: courtesy Kraftmaid

p. 144: © Matthew Gilson, design: Rebekah Zaveloff, KitchenLab, LLC, Design in a Bag, www.designinabag.com

p. 145: © Mark Lohman, design: Gordon Gibson (top left); © Doug Smith, design: Kabira Cadogan, designer, iN/2/iT Design Studio, 515-238-5647 (bottom left); © Matthew Gilson, design: Rebekah Zaveloff, KitchenLab, LLC, Design in a Bag, www.designinabag.com (right)

p. 146: © Eric Roth, design: Robert T. Bowman Builder

p. 147: © Anne Gummerson, design: Joe Architect and Company, Baltimore, 410-908-6753, www.joe-architect.com and Interior Designer Dan Proctor, Kirk Designs, Inc., Baltimore, www.kirk-designs.com (top left); © Eric Roth (top right and bottom left); Eric Roth, design: www.adamsbeasley.com (bottom right)

p. 148: © Eric Roth (left); © Hulya Kolabas, design: CWB Architects (right)

p. 149: © Matthew Gilson, design: Rebekah Zaveloff, KitchenLab, LLC, Design in a Bag, www.designinabag.com (left); © Ryann Ford, design: Paul DeGroot, Architect, www.degrootarchitect.com (right)

p. 150: © Eric Roth, design: www.matthewsapera.com (top); © Ryann Ford (bottom)

p. 151: © Mark Lohman, design: Cynthia Marks Interior Design

p. 152: © Eric Roth (top right and bottom right); © Mark Lohman, design: Cynthia Marks Interior Design (left)

p. 154: © Eric Roth (top); © Eric Roth, design: www.anamikadesign.com (bottom)

p. 155: © Susan Teare, architect: Brad Rabinowitz Architect

p. 156: © Hulya Kolabas, design: Bartels-Pagliaro Architects (top); © Mark Lohman, design: Lynn Pries (bottom)

p. 157: © Susan Teare, design: Elizabeth Hermann architecture + design, Bristol, VT, www.eharchitect.com (left); © Doug Smith, design: Mark Radosevich, MR Construction, Des Moines, IA, 515-225-3577 (right)

p. 158: courtesy Paul DeGrout

p. 159: © Hulya Kolabas, design: Granoff Architecture (left); © Mark Lohman, design: Palm Design Group (top); courtesy Paul DeGrout

p. 160: © Doug Smith, design: Kabira Cadogan, designer, iN/2/iT Design Studio, 515-238-5647 (top left); © Mark Lohman, design: Rohl (top right); © Anne Gummerson, design: Blue Arnold, Kitchens by Request, Jarrettsville, MD (bottom)

p. 161: © Hulya Kolabas, design: Mar Silver Design (left); © Matthew Gilson, design: Rebekah Zaveloff, KitchenLab, LLC, Design in a Bag, www.designinabag.com (top right); © Doug Smith, design: Mark Radosevich, MR Construction, Des Moines, IA, 515-225-3577 (bottom right)

CHAPTER 6

p. 162: © Eric Roth, design: www.trikeenan.com/

p. 164: © Ryann Ford, design: Paul DeGroot, Architect, www.degrootarchitect.com

p. 165: © Eric Roth, design: www.hutkerarchitects.com (top left); © Ryann Ford (top right and bottom)

p. 166: © Eric Roth, design: www.trikeenan.com/ (left); © Ryann Ford, design: Paul DeGroot, Architect, www.degrootarchitect.com (center); © Hulya Kolabas, design: Vicki Taylor-Bloch and Donna Sexton AtHome Design LLC (right)

p. 167: © Eric Roth, design: www.nicholaeff.com

p. 168: © Susan Teare, design: Topcoat Finishes, Red House Building and Trice Strattman Designs (top); © Anne Gummerson, design: Brennan and Company Architects, Ellicott City, MD (bottom)

p. 169: © Matthew Gilson, design: Rebekah Zaveloff, KitchenLab, LLC, Design in a Bag, www.designinabag.com

p. 170: © Eric Roth (top left); © Ryann Ford, design: Paul DeGroot, Architect, www.degrootarchitect.com (top right); © Tria Giovan, design: Phillip Sides (bottom)

p. 171: © Ryann Ford (left); © Matthew Gilson, design: Rebekah Zaveloff, KitchenLab, LLC, Design in a Bag, www.designinabag.com (right)

p. 172: © Eric Roth

p. 173: © Doug Smith, design: Kabira Cadogan, designer, iN/2/iT Design Studio, 515-238-5647 (left); © Ryann Ford, design: Paul DeGroot, Architect, www.degrootarchitect.com (top right); © Doug Smith, design: Mark Radosevich, MR Construction, Des Moines, IA, 515-225-3577 (bottom right)

p. 174: © Eric Roth, design: www.duffydesigngroup.com

p. 175: © Mark Lohman, design: Palm Design Group (left); © Doug Smith, design: Kabira Cadogan, designer, iN/2/iT Design Studio, 515-238-5647 (right)

p. 176: © Eric Roth, design: www.jonathancutlerarchitect.com

p. 177: © Eric Roth, design: www.paynebouchier.com (top left); © Anne Gummerson, design: John Gartling, Innovative Interior Design, Baltimore (bottom left); © Eric Roth, design: www.breesearchitects.com (right)

p. 178: © Matthew Gilson, design: Rebekah Zaveloff, KitchenLab, LLC, Design in a Bag, www.designinabag.com (top); © Eric Roth, design: www.deanporitzky.com (bottom)

p. 179: © Matthew Gilson, design: Rebekah Zaveloff, KitchenLab, LLC, Design in a Bag, www.designinabag.com (left and right)

p. 180: courtesy Armstrong (left and right)

p. 181: © Eric Roth, design: www.charlie-allen.com

p. 182: © Eric Roth, design: theredesign.com

p. 183: © Eric Roth (top left); © Eric Roth, design: www.deanporitzky.com (top right); © Eric Roth, design: www.lizcaan.com (bottom)

p. 184: © Eric Roth, design: CCW Design (left); © Eric Roth, design: www.dressingroomsdesign.com (right)

p. 185: © Eric Roth

p. 186: © Eric Roth

p. 187: © Eric Roth (top); © Hulya Kolabas, design: Lauren Muse Interiors + Christina Murphy Interiors (bottom left); © Eric Roth, design: www.wilsonkelseydesign.com (bottom right)

p. 188: © Susan Teare, design: Peregrine Design/Build

p. 189: © Eric Roth (top left and bottom left); © Eric Roth, design: www.horstbuchanan.com

p. 190: © Eric Roth

p. 191: © Eric Roth, design: www.brittadesign.com (left); © Eric Roth, design: www.christofiinteriors.com

p. 192: © Matthew Gilson, design: Rebekah Zaveloff, KitchenLab, LLC, Design in a Bag, www.designinabag.com (left and right)

p. 193: © Eric Roth, design: www.carpentermacneille.com (left); © Mark Lohman, design: Little Crown Interiors (right)

p. 194: © Tria Giovan, design: Suzanne Kasler (top); © Hulya Kolabas, design: Stacey Gendelman Interior Design (bottom left); © Ryann Ford, design: Paul DeGroot, Architect, www.degrootarchitect.com (bottom right)

p. 195: © Eric Roth

CHAPTER 7

p. 196: © Ryann Ford, design: Paul DeGroot, Architect, www.degrootarchitect.com

p. 198: © Matthew Gilson, design: Rebekah Zaveloff, KitchenLab, LLC, Design in a Bag, www.designinabag.com

p. 199: © Ryann Ford, design: Paul DeGroot, Architect, www.degrootarchitect.com (left and top right); © Eric Roth (bottom)

p. 200: © Doug Smith, design: Mark Radosevich, MR Construction, Des Moines, IA, 515-225-3577

p. 201: © Matthew Gilson, design: Rebekah Zaveloff, KitchenLab, LLC, Design in a Bag, www.designinabag.com (top left and bottom left); © Ryann Ford, design: Paul DeGroot, Architect, www.degrootarchitect.com (right)

p. 202: © Matthew Gilson, design: Rebekah Zaveloff, KitchenLab, LLC, Design in a Bag, www.designinabag.com (top); © Anne Gummerson, design: Rhea Arnot Interior Design, Baltimore (bottom)

p. 203: © Eric Roth

p. 204: © Anne Gummerson, design: Taylor Reed Design-Build, Monkton, MD, 410-343-2100 (left); © Anne Gummerson, design: Blue Arnold, Kitchens by Request, Jarrettsville, MD (right)

p. 205: © Doug Smith, design: Kabira Cadogan, designer, iN/2/iT Design Studio, 515-238-5647 (top left); © Doug Smith, design: Mark Radosevich, MR Construction, Des Moines, IA, 515-225-3577 (bottom left); © Ryann Ford (right)

p. 206: © Hulya Kolabas, design: Mar Silver Design

p. 207: © Doug Smith, design: Mark Radosevich, MR Construction, Des Moines, IA, 515-225-3577 (top); © Matthew Gilson, design: Rebekah Zaveloff, KitchenLab, LLC, Design in a Bag, www.designinabag.com (bottom)

p. 208: © Eric Roth, design: www.carpentermacneille.com

p. 209: © Susan Teare, architect: Brad Rabinowitz Architect (left); © Doug Smith, design: Kabira Cadogan, designer, iN/2/iT Design Studio, 515-238-5647 (right)

p. 210: © Doug Smith, design: Mark Radosevich, MR Construction, Des Moines, IA, 515-225-3577 (left and right)

p. 211: © Ryann Ford, design: Paul DeGroot, Architect, www.degrootarchitect.com (left); © Hulya Kolabas, design: Neil Hauck Architects (right)

p. 212: © Eric Roth

If you like this book,
you'll love *Fine Homebuilding.*

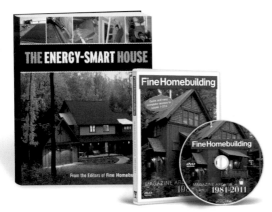